The World Deserves My Children

The World Deserves My Children

NATASHA LEGGERO

GALLERY BOOKS

New York   London   Toronto   Sydney   New Delhi

G

Gallery Books
An Imprint of Simon & Schuster, Inc.
1230 Avenue of the Americas
New York, NY 10020

First Gallery Books hardcover edition November 2022

GALLERY BOOKS and colophon are registered trademarks of Simon & Schuster, Inc.

For information about special discounts for bulk purchases, please contact Simon & Schuster Special Sales at 1-866-506-1949 or business@simonandschuster.com.

The Simon & Schuster Speakers Bureau can bring authors to your live event. For more information or to book an event, contact the Simon & Schuster Speakers Bureau at 1-866-248-3049 or visit our website at www.simonspeakers.com.

Interior design by Jaime Putorti

Manufactured in China

10   9   8   7   6   5   4   3   2   1

Library of Congress Control Number: 2022931839

ISBN 978-1-9821-3707-6
ISBN 978-1-9821-3709-0 (ebook)

To my mother, my children, and my children's children

CONTENTS

CONTENTS

---

* If you're related to me and reading this, read this first!

The World Deserves My Children

INTRODUCTION

I love throwing parties. There isn't an event that I don't think of as an excuse for a party. That might be the one thing I like most about Judaism, i.e., the religion my husband forced me to convert to. Jews have a party where we drink wine, eat bread, and your husband blesses you EVERY FRIDAY NIGHT! (I've always wanted to be blessed weekly.)

I've thrown every kind of party—from a dog's baptism to my own "yard wedding"—so naturally, on the eve of the first woman being elected president, my husband and I agreed we had to throw an epic election (coronation?) party.

Inspired by a trend in Paris of turning public pools into floating movie houses, I rented a huge TV, wheeled it out by my pool, shoveled a bunch of greenhouse gas into the furnace, turned the water up to 101°F, got tons of giant pink inflatable swans that I begged my brother to blow up for me, and had the party catered with my favorite Mexican food. Get it? Mexican food? Trump? Ha-ha?

Like every other liberal idiot I share a bubble with, I *knew* Hillary was going to win. The day what's-his-name was caught on tape saying that he grabs women by the pussy, I actually got annoyed that Hillary's campaign was STILL emailing me asking for money. "Enough, bitch, I think ya got this."

The sound was off on the TV as a bunch of comedians floated in the pool-sized hot tub. I'd made an awesome playlist with inspirational classics like "The Times They Are A-Changin'" and "We Are the Champions." As we lay on the inflatable pool toys, smugly basking in certain victory with our margaritas and mini burritos, the mood started to shift from ironic whimsy to intense dread.

With Lou Reed's "Perfect Day" blaring from the speakers, we noticed Trump had won *another* state. There was less splashing from the pool. Adorable little burrititos started to turn cold. An inner tube shaped like a flamingo frowned.

I decided to get out of the tub, turn down the music, and start asking my smartest, most politically savvy friends what the hell was happening. I was hoping for a "Don't worry, it's about to turn around!" What I got was an "If Trump wins Michigan, there's no way he *won't* win the election." I looked up at the giant screen looming over the chimichanga bar. He won Michigan. The splashing stopped. The margarita machine froze in terror. The flamingo looked like he was going to be sick.

A chill swept over the party. There was silence, which is rarer in a group of comedians than a happy childhood. We were all in shock. Our bubble had been popped. Bewildered and soaking wet, people started getting out of the pool looking for towels. As I waved goodbye to my guests with an air of "Yes, this was a bummer but we will all figure it out tomorrow!" (as I said, I'm a good host), I started picking up unused party horns and poppers that were lying on the tables and thought, *Maybe I won't have a kid.*

I froze my eggs on a whim when I was thirty-eight and I didn't really think I would use them. I didn't even have a boyfriend at the time. I wasn't exactly maternal. I truly believed my classic joke: "Having a baby is like a DUI from the universe."

But still, I had some extra money and thought maybe one day I might want a kid, in the same way I thought I might eventually want an infinity hot tub. (I have one of those on ice too.)

I could definitely live without one, but I thought it might be cute to have a little sidekick to take to the spa and play piano with and who would join me in my Pinot and Painting classes on Wednesdays. Together we would reenact scenes from impressionist masters: mother and daughter rowing in a boat, brushing each other's hair, her lovingly emptying my bedpan and topping off my Château Margaux whenever I got parched.

Every time I thought about it, though, having a kid just seemed like a lot of work. Not to mention it's expensive, majorly cuts into your leisure time, derails your career accomplishments, and destroys your romance with your partner. And despite all these sacrifices, it could still grow up and do makeup tutorials on TikTok.

I also worried that in my future kid's lifetime, it would most likely experience coastal change, increased wildfires, plagues and pandemics, lack of resources due to overpopulation, nuclear war, and, maybe worst of all, more reality-show presidents. How could I bring a child into a world where it would almost certainly one day hear a candidate for president say, "America, will you accept this rose?"

Was it conscionable to have a child when it will just create more pollution in an already pretty full earth that, oh yeah, just happens to be on fire?

I decided that it was. Why should I feel guilty for procreating? Even in the most tragic of times, people were having kids. World War II was the worst catastrophe in modern history, but two weeks after it ended, people were fucking so much that they gave birth to an entire generation of people who are now ruining the world. OK boomer?

The truth is, no matter how bad the world is, people will still be getting married, they will still be having kids, those kids will still be annoying, and there will always be husbands who are completely unhelpful and grandparents who are too frail to watch your kids. You may have to swab your nanny's larynx for viral shedding before she comes to work, but the cycle of life will not stop.

When I decided to thaw my eggs and crack them over the cast-iron griddle of my uterus, I had a husband, a house, and a career, and knew just from gut feeling which parties to attend and which to skip. How unfair would it be if I kept those little frozen potential Leggeros from attending the party that is my life? I decided to become a mom when I was in my prime, but when the world most certainly was not.

That's what this book is about, waiting just long enough to have a child so that you are stable and ready for whatever parenthood throws at you, but not *so* long that you have to give birth in an underground city where oxygen is piped in from the surface and your children think piles of dirt are trees. And if you *do* wait too long? Don't stress! You're literally creating a bunker mate to hang out with you and to eat rehydrated beans with. Who wants to do that alone?

If you're on the fence about the state of the world or your own readiness to raise a child and give up your freedom, do what I did: face the most monumental decision you'll ever make and say, "Hey, fuck it, why not?" In fact, Why Not is the name of my sweet, sweet daughter.*

---

* That's a lie.

SO, WHAT'S IT LIKE BEING A MOTHER?

"Women are troublesome cattle to deal with mostly."
—SAMUEL LOVER, *HANDY ANDY* (1842)

"Woman is not intended for great mental or for great physical labour. She expiates the guilt of life not through activity but through suffering, through the pains of childbirth, caring for the child and subjection to the man, to whom she should be a patient and cheering companion."
—ARTHUR SCHOPENHAUER, "ON WOMEN" (1851)

I've been trying to finish reading a magazine article for seven months. And it's not even from one of the smart magazines people in New York pretend to read on the subway. I've bought six books on my Kindle and have read 0 percent of all of them. (Sorry, Michelle Obama.) I've downloaded all five hundred hours of TV that Ryan Murphy has made in the last six months, but I haven't watched any of it because I go to bed at nine thirty. And I love highly stylized sass.

"So, what's it like being a mother?" my single, childless, thirty-eight-year-old male friend asked over coffee. I'd spent the previous twenty minutes droning on about the minutiae of child-rearing, but I guess he hadn't been listening. . . .

"Can you read a book while watching your baby?" NO. Not unless you want her to fall off a cliff. (I prefer to read on the bluffs above Malibu.) You can't do shit. Your time no longer belongs to you. I tried to explain that having a kid is loving something so intensely that you can't live without it, mixed with desperately wanting that *something* to take a nap so dangerously long that you have to go into its room and check if it's still breathing.

"Sounds like being a mom is hard," he said, in the type of understatement only available to child-free men of a certain age. But then he went a step further. "Sounds like it really takes over your whole life."

That thought panicked me. I don't want my whole life to be taken over. I didn't have a kid to get a new life; I had a kid to enrich the one I already had. I'm not *just* a mom. I've been a human adult for far longer than I've been a mother. What happened to that person?

Before my daughter was born, I spent three years decorating my house exactly how I wanted it. I'd spent a lot of years figuring out what I liked and then a lot more years working hard to be able to afford it. You have to tell a *lot* of jokes to pay for Hermès grass-cloth wallpaper.

I found the perfect fabrics, the perfect furniture, the perfect fixtures. I talked my husband out of every bad decorating idea he had—including building a trash chute that emptied out of the dining room window (*It's like a slide, but for garbage!*)—and I'd won every battle. I didn't need the thousands of Instagram likes to tell me that my house was perfect. (Tens of thousands, if we're being specific.) I had the jealous looks of all my friends in real life to do that.

And then, before I could even dent the cushions in my vintage velvet armchairs, I was being quoted $400 by a man who'd come to babyproof my exquisitely designed, expertly curated, totally and irredeemably child-unfriendly house.

His clipboard was a litany of aesthetic horrors: huge plastic clasps to lock the toilet seat down; a plastic gate bolted into the perimeter of the fireplace; barricades that looked like we were preparing the living room for Occupy Wall Street. Apparently there was no Valentino babyproofing collection. The baby-proofer told me not to worry. The gates could be purple and even have my daughter's name on them. Thank god we had a fainting couch, because I was feeling a touch of the vapors coming on.

I used to hate when someone would ask me a question like, "What are you doing on February second?" And I'd say, "That's three weeks away, how the fuck do I know? I could be living in France!" But now every second of every day is accounted for. If I ever want to do something luxurious, like condition my hair or eat a sandwich, I have to schedule it during my daughter's naps. Well, I have a nanny now. But I have to write this book to pay for her.

I get up at 6 a.m. Which means in order to get my nine hours of beauty rest, I have to go to bed by ten. Nothing *really* fun happens before 10 p.m. Okay, *maybe* a *Nailed It* marathon while deeply comatose from Indian food, with your partner snoring beside you (perhaps I was the one snoring). But that shouldn't be every night.

Now that I've had a baby, I spend nearly 70 percent of my brainpower ruminating on whether or not she is okay. Every second I spend with her, my eyes are glued to her to make sure she doesn't put a switchblade in her mouth. (I'm not giving up my switchblade collection no matter how much I love that baby.)

Is this my new life? Am I just a mom? Am I going to start dressing like a college student who pulled an all-nighter? Is my front yard going to look like a day-care center? Am I going to have to climb over a plastic gate to get into my living room for the next five years? Am I going to be substituting placenta for protein in my stir-fries? (JK . . . I can't cook.)

In 2021 the US birthrate fell to its lowest point in more than a century. And the people who *are* having kids are doing it older and older. Most women I know are having babies later in life. Only Christians and Hasidic Jews are getting married in their twenties. And that's only because they're not allowed to have sex before then.

Our mothers put their lives on hold to raise children, but the paradigm has shifted. Now many of us are having kids well after we develop our personalities. And science has intervened to help. Now you can have frozen-egg babies well into your forties and fifties. It's only a matter of time before a woman in her seventies can do what men in their seventies have been doing forever: become a new parent and/or die of a heart attack during sex with a much younger partner. Your time is now, old ladies!

I waited so long to have a baby because I thought I had to wait to find someone who would split the work with me. I wanted to wait until I found the perfect man. But here's what I didn't understand: as a mother, even with a solid, equal partner, I *still* have to do everything. If you are a straight woman, you have to come to terms with the fact that even if you find the perfect man, he will still be a man. No one knows how to comfort my baby like I do, even when my husband and I trade off mornings.

For example, when it's one of my mornings, here's how it goes: the clock turns six fifteen, the baby cries, and I go to her, pick her up, comfort her, and carry her into the kitchen and make her a bottle.

Here's what it looks like when my partner does it: clock turns six fifteen, baby cries, he grabs his phone, starts vaping, stumbles into the kitchen, *eats breakfast*, makes coffee, and then thinks about starting to make her bottle.

At this point, even though it's my morning "off," I'm not sleeping anymore because my baby is *still* crying! I stumble into the kitchen, yell at my husband, "You're eating Fruity Pebbles while she's crying?" "She's fine," he grunts. And then I go do everything myself.

It's hard raising a child with a man. If what's going on at my house is any indication, the female and male parenting styles are very different. As a mother, I would have to have five drinks and be in a full-body cast for my parenting style to be equal to that of a sober father. I'd say that twice a week my husband asks if we can leave the baby in the car. No, we can't leave the baby in the car. (*"But it's overcast!"*) You don't need the Barnes & Noble baby section to know you can't leave a baby in a car. That's, like, a classic.

One day I asked my husband to give the baby a bath. I came into the kitchen to find my daughter sitting in a sink full of dishes while my husband scrubbed her and a plate at the same time. Don't use Dawn on her! She's a baby, not a duck after an oil spill. I would have to be very drunk to do any of that, so I have no idea what he thinks is normal.

I asked him recently if he knew that it's not okay for him to pick the baby up by the neck, like she's a friendly possum or misbehaving cat. Maybe it was an insulting question, but I just wanted to make sure! He asked me if I think he's a "fucking idiot." (I declined to answer.) Which, by the way, is *not* the same as saying, "Yes, I know that's not okay." So I still don't know.

And now, every other day, right at the baby's bedtime, he's taking karate classes at Pasadena Community College. Is he trying to lose the baby weight? Or maybe he wants to be able to defend his family if we ever find ourselves surrounded by bad guys in a movie from the seventies? He's enrolled in community college to get out of putting her to bed. And it's not just him. I know a male comic who had two high-profile stand-up shows and an appearance on *Conan* by the time his kid was ten days old. DAYS! I don't think I left my bed for two *months* after I gave birth. I still felt my C-section scar throbbing while I delivered jokes onstage a year later. It took my husband a full three days to recover and start pursuing his yellow belt.

There's a lot my husband *doesn't* do: shut drawers, find his wallet, write checks, schedule appointments, put appointments in the calendar, know we have a calendar.

But there are a few things he *can't* do: give birth to a child, nurse a child, break a wood board with his fist. (Still looking forward to that belt ceremony, honey.)

Women are more affected by childbirth than men. That's just a fact. I put a lot of effort into having this thing! (To be more accurate, he had to do ONE thing, and it's one of his favorite things to do.) My husband was certainly supportive, but he didn't actually have to do much.

I'm the one who went on fertility medicine and had to inject hormones in my butt for a year. I'm the one who had to get pregnant. He would have made a better pregnant person than me. He doesn't drink or do drugs, he's disciplined with what he eats. He could've just laid in bed playing *Red Dead Redemption*, never worrying that nobody would hire him because he was fat.

I'm the one who had to deliver the thing! (Although perhaps *deliver* is a generous word. I delivered myself into the loving hands of an obstetric surgeon.) I'm the one who had to feed it from my body. When our baby pulls my husband's chest hair, he screams. Try having a baby sucking on your nipples. Now imagine that baby has two new front teeth!

And I know this will get me in trouble, but nothing made me feel less like my own person and more like "just a mom" than breastfeeding.

I dreaded breastfeeding. While I was still pregnant, so many people told me I would love it that I started to get very suspicious. Usually when everyone loves something, that's a bad sign. Just look at the most popular videos on YouTube.

Every mother I knew kept saying breastfeeding was an amazing bonding experience. I wondered if changing a diaper was also a bonding experience? Even the hospital was very pro-breastfeeding. As you entered the hallways of the recovery rooms, there was a wall of black-and-white photographs of women breastfeeding, and slogans like *Human Milk for Human Babies*.

Many of the nurses who help you in those first twenty-four hours belong to La Leche League, and their life's mission is to remove all shame from breastfeeding. That part I actually loved. I had fantasies about whipping my big fat tit out and having some dude mansplain what's appropriate in a public space and then I'd yell at him, "These are my tits and my baby, and I am proud to feed her in the hair-care aisle at Walgreens."

But that's the only part I was excited for. In the recovery room they didn't really give you an option. The nurses just immediately put the baby on your boob to see if it latched. Well, my baby latched perfectly, and guess what? I hated it! Apparently, I had a lot of milk. People said I should be grateful, that some women barely have *any* milk. Women would kill for the amount of milk I had. I wasn't grateful. I was uncomfortable. I didn't want to have to milk my tits every two to three hours.

Two months or so into my daughter's life, I reached a breaking point.

I was watching a movie across town. My tits started throbbing so hard I couldn't sit there anymore. I had only been away from my baby's mouth for two hours. But my tits didn't care. They just kept pulsing and throbbing. I went to the bathroom and tried to hand-squeeze some milk, to no avail. I left the movie before it was finished and went home to my satanic pump machine and sat staring off into space thinking, *I don't want this to be my life.*

The moment I had to walk out of that very touching Mr. Rogers documentary to milk myself into an ArcLight sink was the moment I realized I'd lost control of my life. And I was ready to take it back.

A little while later, I was sitting at a café with one of my husband's many friends from Burning Man, and she said that breastfeeding is a choice, which I found reassuring. Then she said she only chooses to breastfeed because she doesn't want her kid to get sick. And I do?

Rather than take medical advice from a woman whose idea of fun is spending a week in the desert, wearing body paint and attending seminars about the healing power of dirt, I decided to ask my ob-gyn how long I had to breastfeed. He blew off the question with a wave and said, "A month is fine." Granted, my ob-gyn who delivered my baby is *very* relaxed. He's a gay man who adopted his son from one of his patients, who was already a mother of four and was going to abort it. "I'll take it!" he said, and so she carried it to term and then gave it to him.

After the baby was born, he told me, he hired a woman off Craigslist to stare at it all day and feed it Similac. She ended up being their live-in nanny for eighteen years. And his kid was just fine! But considering he was on the relaxed side of the parenting scale, I decided I would ask my pediatrician as well. They deal more with the babies *after* they come out, while the ob-gyn is more focused on your vagina and getting the thing out of it. So I asked the pediatrician, and she said three months would be a good amount of time for my child to slop up all of the benefits that were flowing from my highly productive milk titties. I'm not sure if that's exactly what she said; I kind of stopped listening after I heard the words "three months." I remember her saying something about the benefits of breast milk being real, but that the amount of time women were expected to breastfeed could be overstated.

For example, if you breastfeed for six months, you can apparently actually reduce your risk of getting breast cancer by 30 percent. I did three months, so maybe I'm halfway there? If there are added benefits to doing it longer, I had a decision to make: Was protecting my child from the dangers of a slightly higher sensitivity to gluten later in life a fair price to pay for nursing her until she's old enough to walk over, pull up my shirt, and serve herself, like my tits are the Dr Pepper fountain at a McDonald's that has free refills? Maybe if you're old enough to *ask* for breast milk, you're too old to drink breast milk?

Breastfeeding was preventing me from getting back to my life. Since it's not Pioneer Days, I have to go make money. I tell jokes for a living and I had to go figure out how to be myself onstage again. But the world isn't set up for a cool working mother. When you give birth, who you thought you were goes away. You've now become something else. A milk dispenser, for one.

Sometimes I wish we were still living in the days when women didn't have to do anything. All I would have to do is lie around dreaming of the career I wasn't allowed to pursue, and if I wanted something from my husband I'd say, "Please, Mr. Sweetie, buy me a dress!" And if he wouldn't buy it for me, I would just pass out onto my newly purchased fainting couch.

Alas, I guess I'm what they call a working mother. And working mothers can't always turn to other mothers for support. Why not, you ask? Well, to put it delicately: other mothers are judgmental bitches.

A lot of them, at least.

So I decided on my own. I stopped breastfeeding. It had been around three months already. I began the process of weaning and contacted a lactation specialist to help me figure out how to stop the avalanche of white gold that was spraying out of my tits every time I left the house.

I was told if I didn't do this correctly, I could get a clogged duct or, worse, an infection. She really wanted me to keep trying to breastfeed, since I had so much milk and my child was latching. But I said I couldn't. I didn't want to be tied to my house and I didn't want to pump. It was annoying and those machines are absurd. I still wake up in a cold sweat some nights thinking about the drone of the pump machine. I wouldn't wish that sound on anyone. Except my husband, who managed to sleep through it every night with the kind of self-discipline reserved only for karate masters.

The lactation specialist emphasized that the benefits were not just for the health of the baby but that it was also an important bonding experience. I told her that when I *was* able to be home breastfeeding, it was a nice bonding experience. But so was giving her a bottle. I mean, that's what fathers do. The whole arrangement felt like a conspiracy to keep you at home, and it's completely impractical for a working woman. Formula was invented for flappers so they didn't have to be home in a kitchen during the Jazz Age. It was a solution! Because of formula, women could enter the workforce, make their own money, and finally hear Duke Ellington sing live. The lactation specialist said it was ultimately my decision and turned over her information. I went on her prescribed regimen, which included stuffing my bra with cabbage.

And now my baby is beautiful and healthy and has gotten the same amount of sick as all of her breastfed-for-two-years brethren, and most of all, now we're *both* happy! The point is, I acted selfishly. I didn't want to breastfeed. I *really* didn't want to pump. And everything turned out fine. And people might read this and judge me. But I don't care. I mean, of course I care, but I'll try to not ruminate on it when you send me hate mail.

No one knows what works, and even when it does work, the kid might still end up hating you, so you might as well do what works for you. Remember: they are joining your life, you aren't joining theirs. By the time you can actually have a stimulating conversation with your kid, they never want to talk to you again. At least, this is what my friends with older kids say.

So why not make your life how you want and they will figure out how to fit in it? Because the truth is that nobody, not the judgey other parents, the experts, the old lady giving parenting advice in line at Vons supermarket, really knows anything about parenting.

Except for the thing about making eye contact with your kids. That one seems important.

MY CHILDHOOD

"My advice to young people? Try to be born in Paris."
—DIANA VREELAND

Los Angeles is filled with bright-eyed people in their early twenties, or as we call them in the entertainment business, "assistants." While they wait patiently for Netflix or Hulu to hand them a ten-episode order for a show based on their web series about dating in the age of Postmates, these whippersnappers keep themselves busy attending to the wants and needs of Hollywood's actors, writers, directors, and, of course, actor-writer-directors.

There's only one problem. No one knows how to do anything anymore. I once asked an assistant to print out a script for me, and she handed me a loose pile of papers. She hadn't stapled them because the stapler was empty, and despite her college degree, she didn't know how to refill a stapler or where to buy staples (one hint: at the store called, helpfully, Staples) or why I even needed staples because who still reads anything on paper? She might just as well have said, "Here's a loose pile of papers, you old piece of shit. Get an iPad, bitch!"

I meet twenty-three-year-olds who need to watch a ten-second video on their phones to figure out how much milk to put in their coffee. Meanwhile, when my father was twenty-three, he had three kids, a job, and a mortgage. It couldn't have been easy. Actually, I know it wasn't easy, because he left. I remember my dad approaching me one day when I was around five, with his dry cleaning over his back. He leaned down to shake my hand and said, "See ya later, kid, I'm leaving." I must've felt this wasn't normal behavior for him, as he usually didn't tell me when he was coming and going, so I said, "Where?" He said he didn't know and also he didn't know when he was coming back. I shrugged, said goodbye, and went back to playing.

My father left his family at twenty-three, but at least he knew how to get his clothes dry-cleaned. I would have hired him as an assistant in a heartbeat.

I grew up in Rockford, Illinois. By the time I was twelve, I had two paper routes, worked in a grocery store, babysat, and mowed lawns (I schlepped my own lawn mower all over town). I even worked the concession stand at the Jewish Community Center (a harbinger of things to come! and also where I learned the word *schlepp*). I often found myself looking at the clock at the grocery store where I worked, wondering when my life would start.

But first, I had to help my now-single mother raise my two younger brothers, one of whom was a "problem child." As soon as he exited my mom's vagina, my brother wanted to get into a beer brawl. He broke a kid's rib on the bus to school, tried to flush the babysitter's head down the toilet, and would attempt to sumo wrestle anyone who came to the house. He hated rules and dedicated his life to doing the opposite of what he was told. My mom told me that when he was a baby, he would want to wear swimsuits in the winter and a parka in the summer. No one knows why he acted this way, but perhaps he wasn't breastfed long enough.

Our house had a detached garage, which my mother always kept locked, her attempt to keep my brother away from the power tools. One day he broke the windows, climbed in, and sawed off his own cast. (He had many casts throughout childhood, but I believe *this* one was from falling off a tree, or possibly a building?) Another time he took off his own braces with pliers. At least then he saved my mother an expensive visit to the orthodontist.

I remember being left in the car one day (back in the eighties, it was universally considered safe for parents to leave kids in cars for any amount of time, for any reason—my husband would have loved it) while my mom was trying to get my brother admitted to the city's only Lutheran school. He had gotten kicked out of all the others, and there were no religions left in Rockford willing to educate my brother.

He must've escaped the meeting because I remember seeing him running naked across the front lawn of the school, his head shaved except for a ponytail on top of his head. This became his signature hairstyle. It was actually a pretty smart thing to do if you didn't want a Christian school to admit you. Show up with the Hare Krishna hairdo!

One morning we woke to find he had mowed FUCK YOU into the lawn, and when we tried to talk to him he just kept barking and acting like a dog for the rest of the day. Another time we had to go visit the farm where my mother grew up, which she'd inherited after her dad's death. We were driving from Ely, Minnesota, back to Rockford and stopped at one of those lookout points at the edge of a cliff. There was a three-foot barrier serving as a gate, separating us from the cliff below. We were taking in the view when all of a sudden my brother flipped himself over the barrier. We heard a loud, echoed scream as he fell to what appeared to be his death. My other brother and I froze in disbelief, my mother turned white, and all of our hearts sank.

There was a very long, horrible silence. And then suddenly, my brother popped back up. "SURPRISE!!!" He must've seen that it wasn't an actual cliff and decided to "surprise" us. My mother broke down and cried for a very long time. No wonder I vowed never to have children.

The daily responsibilities of a parent didn't seem much better. I was in charge of making my brothers' lunches, ironing their uniforms for Catholic school (my brother's stint with the Lutherans lasted only a week), and making them dinner while my mom was at work. My specialty was Lipton Rice Sides as the main meal. (I would ironically serve this with no sides.) I usually don't brag about my cooking, but I'm actually great at making all types of packaged foods. My ability to measure how much water goes into a mixture of powdered cheese and a variety of different shapes of dehydrated starches is unparalleled. I'm also really good at opening up boxes of food. And knowing how long to microwave something. You could say it's a gift. And you probably should.

The moms I saw as a child in Rockford didn't have it easy. The most successful mom I knew was my best friend's. She had a husband and a cleaning lady, instead of being her husband's cleaning lady. She got her nails done once a week and read novels that always had Fabio on the cover. Another friend's mom was a prominent member of Narcotics Anonymous and took in stray dogs, cats, and, occasionally, people. There were always neighborhood kids living in their big house that was on the side of town I wasn't supposed to go to. Another friend slept with her four sisters in a big room with their parents. When their parents weren't sleeping behind the divider of their studio apartment, they were gone following this band I didn't even know I hated yet called the Grateful Dead. My punishment for judging them all those years ago was eventually marrying a man who hasn't missed a Burning Man festival since 2014.

Moms were all around me, and the best of them looked like they had boring lives and the worst seemed to have racked up so many bad decisions that their punishment appeared to be having to be one of my friends' parents.

It wasn't any better for the grandmothers. My grandma had seven kids, so she was pregnant more of her adult life than not.

She also divorced my grandpa more than once because he hit her. It was a different time, I guess. And Italian women were lucky in the seventies because the big glasses they would wear to cover up their bruises were in style and probably didn't attract that much attention.

Of all the moms I knew, my stepmom was the meanest. I'm like Cinderella, if she were a short Italian with dimples.

We would visit my dad on the weekends. My brothers and I and my dad didn't like her kids. It was like *The Brady Bunch* but dysfunctional. Perhaps a mutual dislike for each other's children is what drew them together. (Talk about a meet-cute!) I'm sure part of it was that she used to be my mom's best friend. They grew up together, remained friends into adulthood, and then as soon as my mom and dad got divorced, she married him. I guess she wanted some of that dysfunction for herself. I remember telling my mom that she didn't keep house and there was always food in their sink. I guess I thought this would make my super-clean mom feel better? One night when we were staying with my dad, my stepmom was making chicken with rice and gravy for dinner; when it came time to serve me and my brothers, she said, "Kids don't get to eat meat," and just let us eat rice and gravy. I mean, I liked eating rice for dinner anyway so this wasn't that much of a punishment. I'm not sure if she really believed that kids shouldn't eat meat or she was just being "funny."

She and my dad would fight constantly when we visited, much like how I remembered my parents fighting when my dad lived at home. My stepmom would sit at the dining room table in the morning with a box of wine and a cigarette dangling from her mouth. (In Rockford, this combination is called a Grand Slam Breakfast. I think that's where Denny's got the name.) It never occurred to me that she didn't do this every day, but now that I think about it, she was probably protesting our visit. Or maybe this was how she partied on the weekend? I would actually like to day-drink in the dining room on a Saturday morning and give anyone who talks to me the stink eye. But even as a child I didn't understand why she had a box of chardonnay on the table. It should obviously have been in the refrigerator.

I think my mom wanted a different life for me. So she took me to the Y.

In Rockford, the YMCA was the epicenter of white trash entertainment. I started taking swim lessons there when I was three. I was later on the swim team all throughout high school with my best friend, Lynn, because our moms *made* us do it. I imagine if moms gave kids a choice of either waking up an extra two hours early in the Illinois winter to swim laps for an hour before school started or to not do that, there would be no one on the swim team. I still remember having wet, crisp hair until lunchtime all throughout high school.

I was a terrible competitive swimmer. I literally never beat anyone. I still have an album of all my yellow (last place) ribbons. They used to put me in the IM because I could do butterfly well enough to technically not get disqualified. (Hence the yellow ribbons. In the eighties, there were no participation ribbons, just kids left alone in the backseats of American-made station wagons while their mothers begged a series of priests and reverends to educate their difficult son.)

The IM stood for "individual medley," which sounded like a frozen food people in Rockford ate. The IM was a few laps of every stroke: back, breast, freestyle, and butterfly. I could never compete with those broad-shouldered Midwesterners who excelled in this sport, but I did know how to do the strokes and had the stamina to finish. I wasn't just last place; I was last place by a mile. I remember at the swim meets, the first-, second-, and third-place swimmers (and the crowd) would be waiting for me to finish in awkward silence. Even though everyone knew I was the worst, I really didn't give a shit, because who wants to be good at competitive swimming? Have you ever had a conversation with a competitive swimmer? I rest my case.

To this day, I still don't understand one thing. WHY IS SWIMMING A SPORT in a town where the temperature routinely gets below zero? They should do competitive sweater bundling. Or sauna-ing. But I'd venture a guess no one in Rockford in 1985 had ever heard of a sauna.

One day my mom was in line at the Y to sign me up for MORE swim classes. Then, by divine intervention, they said the classes were all full. There was, however, an opening in the local theater classes. My mom still needed something to do with me after school, so she signed me up. I don't remember much from the class, but a few months later I got called to the principal's office of St. James Elementary. Someone had been calling looking for the girl in the Catholic school uniform who took acting classes at the YMCA. Yes! That was me! They needed a kid for one of their plays and had tracked me down. Turns out, my acting teacher's brother was the director of the New American Theatre. And just like that, I was recruited to be the resident child in the regional theater in Rockford, Illinois.

If you don't know, a regional theater is a theater company that comprises half professional actors and half amateur/delusional townspeople like myself. Seems like a challenging way to keep standards high, but what did I care? I was hanging out with elderly gay men, bored single women who got manicures, and all types of badly dressed, down-on-their-luck professional actors in the Actors' Equity Association from Chicago. I got to skip school to perform at Wednesday matinees, and now all my evenings were spent at rehearsal instead of cooking microwaved delicacies for my brothers. My first crush was on a thirty-eight-year-old actor in the middle of a divorce.

I always say I was a "child actor," not a "child star." I was the go-to kid for every show. Sometimes the director would write a kid into *As You Like It* just so I could be around. No harm in making changes to Shakespeare, right?

Everybody loved me. There would be months in between the shows when I had to wait it out like a normal child and go back to more school and there'd be no special treatment, and I hated it.

Like an actress who'd made it in the movies but still wanted to be taken seriously, I clung to the idea of "returning to the theater!" with hyperventilating cries to anyone who would listen. The theater was filled with adult talk and culture. I was so confident from acting with professional actors, some of whom had actually LIVED IN NEW YORK, that I was pretty sure Juilliard would accept me based only on my headshot. (Spoiler alert: they did not.)

I learned a lot from being a part of that theater. I mean, not how to act, obviously. While it wasn't exactly Stella Adler, I learned an attitude, and a point of view that gazed out beyond my small town.

I remember discovering sarcasm from my fellow thespians, forty-five-year-old actors going through midlife crises. I would go back to school and share the new words I was learning at the theater. Whenever a teacher went to the bathroom (smoke break) and left the kids alone (why were kids always being left alone in those days?), I'd explain to everyone how Blanche from *The Golden Girls* was a total "slut" and probably had a "loose vagina." I have a vague memory of being dragged out from under a table in my Brownie uniform, pointing and yelling at each girl's underwear under the table: "YOU have a vagina! And YOU have a vagina!" Like a young Oprah, surprising my entire audience with new cars.

I also thought abortion was hilarious. I remember this girl at Catholic school passed out an antiabortion pamphlet that included diary entries that an unborn baby wrote to her mother on each of the seven days before she aborted her. It ended with the entry: "July

10th: Today my mother killed me." That's what we call in my business a *kicker*. I was twelve and couldn't stop laughing. That's probably when I realized I liked darkness. Or maybe I just thought it was funny to imagine a fetus holding a pencil and stationery?

My mom was a thirty-five-year-old single mother of three kids in Rockford, but she managed to save me from a life as a cashier in the Rust Belt by tirelessly driving me to enough extracurricular activities to find something that really spoke to me. And for all I learned in Rockford about what *not* to do as a mother (e.g., don't leave my daughter alone in the car), that's one parenting lesson I'm thankful my mother taught me.

I just hope they have Lyft for babies soon, because I have no intention of driving my kid to ballet practice four days a week in the Simi Valley.

MY CHILDLESS ADULTHOOD

"I'll never be pregnant . . . for long."
—NATASHA LEGGERO

t forty-two, I had already spent two childbearing decades child-free. My lack of offspring was no accident. I wasn't just child-free, I'd been actively trying not to get pregnant since I learned how women got pregnant. (By kissing a man they loved.)

My mom had me when she was twenty-three. It was typical for the time and the place, but it wasn't what I wanted for my life. When I was in my early twenties, a con artist twenty years my senior asked me to sell all of my earthly belongings, give up my rent-stabilized apartment in Manhattan, and move to Australia with him. And I said, "Okay." Your twenties and thirties are filled with decisions like that.

It never made sense to me that you were supposed to spend your two most fun decades nursing children and staying out of executive roles in the workplace. Some women may be able to do it all, but I'm lazy.

Now, at forty-two, my life was finally exactly where I wanted it. And it had only taken me two decades to get there.

After graduating from acting conservatory (not acting school, thank you very much; conservatory is something you attend from 7 a.m. to 7 p.m., while acting school is something you do on Wednesday nights as you try to figure out how to monetize your TikTok), I spent my very early twenties walking around New York literally knocking on casting directors' doors. (This was decades before COVID, when people still worked in offices with doors that you could knock on.) Every casting office would have a bin outside the door with a sign that read: "Actors, please drop your headshots here," making sure all of the unrepresented losers would stop trying to come into their office without an appointment. (They meant me.)

I didn't have a clue how to become a working actor, and it didn't help that I was the most successful actor I knew. Unlike many of my fellow alumni from Stella Adler, I actually had a credit: I was an understudy for one of the waitresses in *Tony n' Tina's Wedding* off-off-Broadway. Important note: There are no waitresses in the cast. This was for an actual waitress for the crowd in attendance, taking antipasto orders from the audience. It was essentially an unpaid waitressing gig, but at least the word *Broadway* was on my résumé.

I was an aggressive, clueless, desperate, out-of-work/had-barely-ever-worked actor. The perfect combination! I would accost famous people if they came into the bar where I worked. I was cocktail-waitressing at the Whiskey Bar in New York when an actress walked in whom I remembered from the summer I spent as a teen watching *Days of our Lives*. My heart began beating loudly and my body began shaking. This was my chance!

She was seated at one of the "reserved" couches, and I pranced over to her in my Whiskey Bar–mandated catsuit. By the way, all of the tables were "reserved," which meant when anyone who wasn't George Clooney sat down, you had to tell them the "reserve" policy, which was more or less "Hey, you guys can sit here for now but if the reservation—i.e., someone more famous than you—comes in, I'm gonna have to move you."

There would be no such speech for this actress; we were about to forge a connection. I told my fellow waitress I would take the table and walked over to the actress, who was seated on a low couch. I kneeled down to her level and told her the seat was technically "reserved" but she could have it because I was a huge fan. I then asked her, while still on my knees, if she would make sure the casting director of *Days* would look at my headshot. She was very sweet and immediately wrote what was no doubt her business manager's address on a napkin and told me to send it to her there and she would make sure the casting person saw it and also that she would like a vodka tonic.

I'm not proud of this behavior, and maybe if Blythe Danner were my mom or I went to a fancy college that had mentorships, I wouldn't have acted like such a fucking idiot the first years of my career, but that was not my fate. I was, in a nutshell, a hick. Ahh, well, those were the days of our lives.

In addition to "pounding the pavement," i.e., bum-rushing the offices of casting directors and agents, I also spent a lot of time in New York in Kinko's (to cut and staple my résumés to my photos), post offices (to mail my résumés and photos), and video stores (to check my email). And then one day it happened: I actually got a response from an agent.

His name was Al Flannigan. I looked him up and he was legit: he repped working actors (not just waitstaff) in New York. I went to his office (overdressed of course), which had a view of Midtown, and I performed a monologue. He liked it and told me to come back the next week to do the monologue for the other agents in the office. I walked out of there and was floating. I couldn't believe it was happening. Would I actually have an agent? Someone who would get me a legitimate time slot for my auditions so I didn't have to just show up and beg for someone to see me or scream the lines from the sidewalk below? I couldn't believe my almost-luck.

I went back the next week and the other agents were in the room waiting. I performed the same monologue: Darlene from *Balm in Gilead*. It went even better than when I had done it for Al. I can be hard on myself, but I couldn't believe how well it went. Even with the pressure of the other agents scrutinizing me, I was able to channel all my angst and desperation into Darlene. They all said they liked it and Al, smiling, told me to call him after

3 p.m. and he would let me know. I walked out of there even higher than the last time.

I went to a pay phone in the lobby of Hunter College, where I was taking a theater criticism class, and waited for the clock to strike three. At 3:01, I called and asked for Al. He told me what a great job I did, but that after discussing it with his colleagues, they had all come to a decision: I was too short to make it as an actress.

I was shell-shocked. He went on to say that while there were some short actress exceptions, like Holly Hunter, in their opinion it probably wouldn't work out for me. I think it was his matter-of-factness that brought me to my knees, heavily sobbing at the pay phone wall at the Hunter College student center. I thanked him for his time in between heaves, hung up the phone, and dropped back to my knees. Al's prophecy that I would never "make it" rendered me barely able to walk. (See, I do have a flare for the dramatic, Al!) I somehow made it home, but Al Flannigan lived inside my head for the next decade, always telling me I would never make it because of something I couldn't control.

I didn't give up. I figured if New York wouldn't have me, I'd go to LA. At least then when I walked around to the casting offices uninvited, I wouldn't be wearing platform shoes in the snow. Also, 9/11 had just happened and I was definitely down for a change of scenery. At the time, I lived in a studio apartment on 138th Street with two windows facing a brick wall. My main décor was a broken antique piano. A friend of a friend knew someone who was getting rid of a piano, and all I had to do was get movers to move it to my place. When the moving men got to my place, they had to disassemble the piano to get it up the steps of my four-story walk-up, and they weren't able to figure out how to put it back together once it was in my apartment. So, for a year I lived in a dark studio in Harlem with a two-piece broken piano. Even if it had been assembled, I didn't know how to play, which made it even more depressing.

Somehow by the grace of the corporate overlords, my bank sent me a letter saying they had put $5,000 in overdraft protection into an account for me, which I could immediately start writing checks from. I never applied for this money, so I called the bank to make sure this wasn't some scam. They confirmed they were lending me $5K. Even if I had known at the time that this $5K would eventually turn into $9K at the high interest rate they were offering (it actually was sort of a scam, as it turns out) and that I would spend a decade in LA paying it back, I still would've accepted it. I immediately started writing checks and mailing them to LA to begin my life there.

I made plans to crash with a friend from the Whiskey Bar who'd moved to LA. I wrote a check to Rent-a-Wreck for a Ford Festiva fresh from a passenger-side accident and even got American Airlines to accept a check for a flight, since I didn't have a credit card. I left New York a week after the bank filled my account with fake money. I didn't even sell my furniture. I invited the building to come descend upon my things, and as the neighborhood kids immediately started defacing my antique vanity and tearing apart my play collection, I got the hell out of New York. The bank paying me to leave Manhattan was one of the only strokes of luck I had received the whole time I was there. I wanted to be a part of it, top of the list, a number one, but all I had to show for my life in New York was a broken piano.

I got some low-level agent who must've specialized in short actresses pretty quickly in LA and immediately started auditioning. Having come from the Stella Adler conservatory and reciting the opening monologue to *Romeo and Juliet* with a cork in my mouth for two years, I would go to auditions speaking in a transatlantic accent. I would go to a commercial audition dressed in my tightest black dress, platform shoes, and detachable boa. I didn't really fit in. I dressed like a heroin addict from the thirties and spoke like Bette Davis: "Try Bud Light, it has drinkability, darling!"

One thing I did notice while out auditioning was that the comedians I met in the waiting rooms were way cooler than the actors. The actors' personalities always sucked: vain, competitive, self-centered. At least comedians knew how to hide these qualities in themselves (and they were funny). I decided I should take an improv class. Well, not just one. If there was a class that had ANYTHING to do with comedy and it was within a fifteen-mile radius (sorry, Orange County sketch-writing classes), I signed up for it.

If there are any budding comedians reading this book, that was probably the crux of my early comedy philosophy: spend every waking hour and all leisure time emerged in comedy. I filled up my schedule with classes. It was like college, where your grades were based 50 percent on making your classmates laugh and 50 percent on resisting those same classmates' attempts to recruit you into Scientology. (Please don't murder me for that joke, Church of Scientology. I'm a mother!)

I waitressed and took any and every class anyone mentioned. I was even in an acting class with Paris Hilton BEFORE she was Paris Hilton; at the time, she was just a great actress.

I knew who she was—some rich person's daughter—because I read *Town & Country* and always looked at what the rich people were doing in any Society section. She came to class the first day with an 8x10 photo album of herself to pass around. She gathered all the students around her with her even-then-signature sweetness and told us about each picture, which were all pictures of herself. As the baffled teacher waited to start class, she held court. "This is me at my birthday party in Tokyo, here I am in Milan . . . ," etc. And I remember the book ended with a photo of her in lingerie. The girl sitting next to me nudged me and asked, "Who the hell is this chick?"

Let me add that bringing a photo album of yourself was not on the syllabus for the Acting for Sitcoms class, but I admired it. She was fascinated by her life and honestly, so was I. Every time she talked, the teacher looked like he was holding in a spit take. She truly had an amazing quality. She was so sweet and innocent and breezy, and you could tell she really believed she was spreading love by showing us pictures of herself at all of the different stops on her international birthday tour. It was like she was sorry we couldn't make it to Tokyo with her, even though she didn't even know us yet, so she brought us back a picture of her as a souvenir, almost like it was the next best thing. In a way, it was like she was including us in her fabulous life.

For one lesson, the teacher asked each student to take a turn sitting in front of the class while the rest of us called out traits that might help them understand their typecasting for sitcoms. This girl Sandy went first. She got up and we started shouting things out to her. "Sandy looks like she would drive fast cars!" "Sandy looks like a rebel!" Paris raised her hand and said proudly, "Sandy likes to sell seashells by the seashore!"

The class was kind of quiet, stunned by Paris's . . . let's say . . . creative? use of childhood tongue-twisters. Yes, Paris, Sandy does sell seashells by the seashore. She sure does. From that moment forward I made it my mission to be friends with Paris Hilton, as I could tell she was going to be huge.

Every week we had class, Paris was getting more and more famous. Then one day I got a call from her social secretary: Paris wanted me to come to her birthday party in Las Vegas. I was so excited. I pictured an intimate gathering in a hotel suite; there'd be some interesting people, maybe a few more 8x10s of Paris in various countries. I got a fellow waitress to come with me to Vegas in her car, as I didn't think my Festiva would make it.

When we got to the hotel, I marched up to the bouncer to inform him that I was on the Paris Hilton guest list. The bouncer pointed to a line wrapped around the casino. I told him again that we were on a list and he said, "So are they," and nodded his head to the line. He also told me I couldn't bring the bottle of wine I had brought for Paris as a present.

Humbled but not discouraged, we got on the back of the line and waited. When we finally got into the "party," I kept asking waitresses where Paris was. Someone pointed to a VIP area guarded by a wall of bouncers dressed in matching Sean John; behind them, Paris sat on a couch with her sister, waving to her public. Other people she'd invited were trying to get her attention, screaming to her between the bouncers as she smiled and continued her royal wave like she was on a parade float. The bouncers told me I wasn't allowed in Paris's area, so she never saw me despite my calls of "Paris! Over here! I brought you merlot! The bouncers confiscated the bottle, but I did bring it!"

I finally put together that Paris had part-ownership in the club and I was just another email she had given to her social secretary to try to fill up the place. I told you I was a hick.

Two years into my LA waitressing residency, I saw a fellow Stella Adler alumni, Melanie Vessy, in the Belly Room of the Comedy Store doing stand-up. I knew she was an actress, and she was so funny that I thought maybe I could do stand-up in front of everyone, too. She told me she took Adam Barnhardt's stand-up comedy "intensive." "A class?" I said. "I can absolutely do that."

Adam's class was cool because there wasn't really a class. You just stood up in front of everyone and talked about your day. It was brilliant, actually. People always make fun of taking classes for stand-up because stand-up comedy can't really be taught. But Adam's class was different. He wasn't telling you what kind of comedian to be or what to write jokes about or what props to use onstage (watermelons and a giant mallet, obviously).

We just talked. We took turns talking into a mic to five other people for four consecutive Mondays until our big show in the Belly Room. I was terrified, so even though I agreed to do the showcase, I didn't invite anyone except the one clingy guy I was having sex with.

I figured I could always back out. I wasn't a stand-up comedy fan at the time. I mean, I knew about Rodney Dangerfield and loved *Seinfeld*, but I had only been to, like, two comedy clubs in my life. I thought stand-up comedians were exclusively men in suits talking about how they didn't get respect and asking what the deal was with various things. I think it was very lucky that before I went on stage for the first time, I hadn't seen any of the great comedic minds who were out there in the LA scene in the early 2000s—Tig Notaro, Sarah Silverman, Laura Kightlinger, Bonnie McFarlane, Jen Kirkman, Morgan Murphy, Maria Bamford, Mary Lynn Rajskub, to name just a few. Having seen them before that probably would have killed my confidence, and I would have canceled my showcase.

My strategy for writing my first set was mostly to keep that clingy boyfriend out of my apartment that weekend. The show was on a Monday, so that Friday I told him he had to spend the next two days at his house.

I locked the door to my studio apartment in Little Armenia, sat on the bed, and started writing topics. I forced myself to write a page on each topic, and the next day I picked my favorites and put them in an order. Then I spent the following day memorizing it. I finally opened the door to my apartment to take out the trash on Sunday, and my clingy boyfriend had left a tray of food outside my door. Cute but not *not* creepy.

For three days I focused on that set and nothing else. I had no contact with the outside world—this was pre-smartphone. If I had wanted to check my email, I would've had to walk to the video store. When Monday night came around, I smoked a few cigarettes and left for the Comedy Store to talk about using men for dinner, dogs off leashes, and poor customer service. I decided against the vintage dress and red leather cap, as I didn't want to bomb dressed like Mary Tyler Moore. I wore dark colors so if I bombed and had to slip out, I might do so unnoticed.

Well, I didn't bomb. I actually had the best set I've ever had STILL TO THIS DAY, I think partly because I couldn't believe people were laughing at things I had written down in my studio that weekend. And they kept laughing. And I kept being surprised/elated by this. Their laughter had a visceral effect on me: it felt like waves rushing over me, and as soon as I came up for air, another wave of laughter would envelop me.

Thinking back, I now realize that feeling was probably the effects of the half an Ambien I forgot I took right before showtime. My hairdresser had given me one "in case of an emergency," and I was so nervous I had taken it before the show. At the time, it didn't occur to me that the intense physical reaction I was having onstage was in fact drug-induced. I got off the stage with a clear direction: I needed more of this. How lucky that for me, "this" was stand-up and not a pill addiction. My luck was turning around.

I never stopped banging on doors—figuratively, at least; I'm thankfully past hustling down Hollywood Boulevard with a stack of headshots under my arm—and working hard to make it as a comedian and actress, and eventually I got to a place where I could pretty much do whatever I chose. It was amazing: I got paid to talk, I could go out every night, and I knew how to keep my overhead down if I ever wanted to take a year off from being paid to talk and instead just spend that time sitting in my perfectly designed home admiring my collection of evening gloves and vaping. (This was before the pandemic, when spending a year inside your house sounded like the height of luxury and not a death-defying necessity.)

But I never took that year off; what I chose to do was riskier, more demanding, and potentially even worse for my career than reprising my role as a waitress delivering Caesar salads to people watching a play I am not even in. What I chose to do was get pregnant.

FORTY-TWO AND PREGNANT
(FREEZE YOUR EGGS)

"The only constant in life is change."
—HERACLITUS

One of the secret perks of becoming a successful actor right away is that you can start a family when you're still really young. I was into my thirties by the time I felt established enough to even think about anything besides my career. Meanwhile, Reese Witherspoon has a twenty-three-year-old daughter. Forget winning an Oscar—there's no greater status symbol for an actor in her forties than an adult child.

I never wanted to have kids. It seemed annoying, and I didn't want to give up my career to raise them. I always thought of my career as my child anyway. I cared about it more than anything, it gave me a reason for living, and at times I was very disappointed in it. My therapist called me a situational breeder. If the right situation arose, maybe I would procreate. I could also be pretty fulfilled if I skipped it.

Getting pregnant for the first time at forty-two can be a little dicey. The technology allowing women to get pregnant in their peak earning years is pretty new. In fact, in-vitro fertilization is itself only about forty-four years old. In other words, IVF would need IVF to get pregnant.

At any rate, it seemed foolish not to freeze my eggs on the off chance that someday I might change my mind. Why *not* freeze them? It cost me nothing to do it (well, I mean, it actually cost me $8,500, but psychologically, it was free).* And it gave me options for the future. Why not keep your options open when you might change your mind someday? I never wanted to get a tattoo for the same reason. What if I had followed through with getting my first boyfriend's name tattooed on my bikini line? Nothing against him, but I'm glad it doesn't say "Bill" in cursive right above my C-section scar. It's the same way with children. Who knows how you're going to feel about things in a decade? Besides, I didn't have to use the eggs. I figured the eggs would just sit in the doctor's freezer, and maybe when I turned seventy I could inject them into my veins like stem cells, or whatever Elizabeth Taylor's doctors were doing to her before she died.

Some unsolicited advice: definitely freeze as many rounds as you can afford. When I froze mine, my doctor explained to me

---

* It cost me $8,500, but you might have to adjust for inflation.

that I'd produced eight eggs that round. I thought that meant I could have eight children, and I barely wanted one. What I didn't realize was that during the freezing, unfreezing, invasive testing, and husband turning them into embryos, you could lose a lot of them, if not all. I later learned I had less than a 30 percent chance of one of these eight eggs even turning into a child.

Sidenote: Donor eggs are more common than you think. Every time you hear a news story like "Miracle Twins at 48" or "Woman Defies All Odds with Baby at 60!" what they don't tell you is that these "miracle babies" are from donor eggs. These aren't miracles, they are purchases. It actually gives people false hope.

In its own way, advances in fertility medicine have been as revolutionary for women as the pill. Now women are free not only to not get pregnant when we don't want to but also to try to get pregnant when we do. I wish I could go back in time and tell all the women throughout history: "You can still have a family—you don't need to have kids with whatever loser you're dating when you're twenty-three."

Actually, I don't need to go back in time to do that. I can just call my mother.

Fertility medicine is amazing. But it's not foolproof.

As my male doctor just couldn't wait to tell me, any pregnancy after thirty-four is considered a "geriatric pregnancy." Yes, geriatric. Geriatric as in "relating to old age." As in "No, I'm not pregnant, this is just my lumpy old flesh." As in "No, these diapers aren't for my baby, they're for me." For those of you writing term

papers about your great-grandmother's exciting life during World
War II, here are a few synonyms for *geriatric*:

> *ancient*
>
> *elderly*
>
> *old*
>
> *senior*
>
> *aged*
>
> *venerable*
>
> *gnarled*
>
> *wizened*

You know, a woman in her thirties.

The man who first shared this lovely turn of phrase with me
said "geriatric pregnancy" so much, I started to think it was his
porn search term. (I mean, it's certainly *somebody's* search term.) I
guarantee that it wasn't a woman doctor who coined the phrase.
It's so like a man to convince women that their childbearing years
are over at thirty-four and that they are geriatric by the time a man
the same age could just be getting into grad school or starting to
"get serious about dating" or finally taking karate lessons.

By the time I was forty-two, my husband and I had been trying for a while. My doctor urged me not to use my frozen eggs just
yet, as he thought there was still a chance I could get pregnant
without them, and recommended my husband and I try IVF (i.e.,

injecting myself with hormones while my husband masturbated in a cubicle at a medical office park in Redondo Beach).

IVF sucks. You're basically turned into Arnold Schwarzenegger injecting steroids à la *Pumping Iron*, but instead of getting jacked, you're getting increasingly hormonal and insane. You know how women are constantly called "crazy" by men who can't handle them? Well, IVF is basically twice-daily injections of a hyperconcentration of crazy-woman juices. You get swollen physically and emotionally. Eventually I needed to enlist my husband's help with the injections, and I could see the pain in his eyes every time he had to slam a needle into one of the main reasons he married me, my perfect Italian ass. It was now covered in injection site bruises and pinpricks. He would look up after injecting me with a tear in his eye. "Mama mia! Whassa happening to *mi preziosa culo?*" He's not Italian, but you get the picture. So, IVF is a wringer, emotionally and physically. It's science intervening in your body's internal transition into its "crone phase," when your ovaries dry up and turn to hot cocoa powder. These injections are a shock to your system—a chemical boost to the old factory workers in your fallopian tubes who, after a lifetime on the egg assembly line, were just about to start collecting their pensions. The injection is a rousing speech by the foreman screaming to the old fellas in egg production: "Come on, guys! I know we are tired. I know we want nothing more than to kick back and enjoy retirement, but she needs us! She only has one more chance to pump out a last batch of eggs!

Who cares if the eggs come out wrinkled or dried up. We can do this!"

The egg assembly line tries to produce new eggs from old equipment—it's a last-ditch effort. For some it can be a miracle procedure; for us, it really didn't work. Not only was it physically painful, emotionally taxing, and totally ineffective, it was also very expensive. Finally we'd had enough and decided to thaw out my eggs on ice (also the name of my favorite ice-skating show).

I had fourteen eggs. Eight survived the thawing process. Then they poured my husband's jizz on them (I assume this is the name of the procedure) and six survived the weight of his load (he wanted me to call it that). Then they tested the embryos for genetic disorders and four survived the procedure. Then we implanted Embryo #1—we'll call him "Bruce." Fail. Then we implanted Embryo #2—we'll call her "Cher."

. . .

. . .

Boom! Pregnant. My husband and I got so excited. It had worked! We went for a spa weekend to relax, and I made the fateful mistake of getting a massage. A week later I miscarried. The doctor told me gently that it was a tubal pregnancy, which is basically when the embryo implants itself into your fallopian tube and fools your body into thinking it's pregnant. It never had a chance. Sure, yeah, but what about that blog I read that said you should avoid massage when pregnant? Was it that? Never mind the medical doctor telling me the pregnancy never had a physical possibility of being successful, I knew—somehow we'd done something wrong.

We were down to one. One last shot. The doctor warned us that each embryo has an approximately 30 percent chance of success. The odds were against us. We started to rethink the future—perhaps we'd just take lots of trips to Europe; Viking River Cruises could be our children! We took a deep breath and I implanted the last one. One last shot that turned into our new roommate for the next eighteen years.

I had already had one miscarriage and was down to a final embryo made from an egg I'd frozen as a thirty-eighth birthday present to myself.

If I didn't get pregnant, I didn't have a very good backup plan. I was forty-two with a husband who didn't want to adopt (he'd had a bad experience with his rescue chihuahua, Pablo). The fear was palpable. And not just because Pablo's shock collar was out of batteries and he was biting everything that moved.

We were fortunate. My husband successfully brought himself to orgasm in his cubicle, I was given twilight anesthesia, and when I woke up, I had a juice box and a geriatric pregnancy. That geriatric pregnancy turned into my very not geriatric baby. My new reason to live. My daughter. My world. Everything had worked out. But the fear wasn't gone. In fact, it was just beginning.

Being a mother seemed like the end to all fun. As one of my friends, a forty-eight-year-old bachelor, told me when I got pregnant, "See you in eighteen years." Parenting is planning. Not having children is freedom. Why would I want to give that up?

For example, travel has always been everything to me. Maybe you want to be the type of parent who takes their toddler to Morocco ("I didn't see a proper casbah until I was thirty-four; I will *not* subject Baby Jasper to such cultural deprivation"), but do you actually want to take a toddler to Morocco? I have a friend who sleep-trained her baby (i.e., let her cry it out) at bed-and-breakfasts across the Northeast one winter. That all sounds terrible to me, but to each their own.

And it wasn't just me who didn't want to give up what I loved: my husband hadn't missed a Burning Man in seventeen years. That's an entire childhood's worth of Burning Man!

I was also under the pretentious delusion that my art was my contribution to the world. Stephen Sondheim even wrote a song about it. (I was his muse.) In *Sunday in the Park with George*, the great pointillist painter Georges Seurat sings a song called "Children and Art." In this delightful marriage of word and sound, Seurat explains there are two ways one can contribute to the world: children and art. It didn't seem like a tough choice to me. Art doesn't get diarrhea or drink from your tits, so I chose art.

And what if I had a kid but then I didn't even like them? Hollywood is full of stories of career-driven women who didn't really want to be mothers once they had kids. Shirley MacLaine's daughter said her mother put her on a plane by herself to Japan when she was two years old and she saw her mother only on holidays and summers. How did I know I wasn't going to do something like that? I'd love to see Tokyo in the winter.

I was famous for having parties that said "No Babies" on the invitation. It was my only rule: "No Babies," as in "No Kids," as in "I don't like your kids." And I don't. I hate other people's kids. I don't really like their pets either. How could anyone but an owner think it's cute to see a cat lick its butt on the kitchen table? I think it's gross. And I feel the same way about your child.

But then I met a man who I thought would be a cool dad. And I thought that he and I could maybe raise a pretty cool child together, and maybe that child would be even more of a contribution to the world than my seventy-three appearances on *Chelsea Lately*. (Art takes many forms.) And suddenly I wanted something more than the opportunity to go out every night and/or be swindled in the outback.*

So we overcame our fear of throwing our perfect lives in the trash for the perfect stranger living inside of me. But a new fear had emerged. My husband was afflicted first.

The very day we learned my pregnancy was going to take, he was diagnosed with FOBB. Fear of Being Basic is a condition that afflicts many former cool people: ex-ravers, onetime punk rockers, art students, college dropouts, bohemians, and people who've been to Burning Man seventeen times in a row.

It's not unreasonable. How can you expect to have the joie de

---

* See chapter 5, Not Partners.

vivre that comes from being a free adult if you're going to have to spend the next eighteen years unable to leave your house without making childcare plans (not to mention paying for those plans, as we will discuss in a later chapter about nannies, babysitters, and day care, or all of the potential alcoholics, drug addicts, and sex offenders you pay to watch your child so you can be an adult for ten minutes).

As the partner of a person suffering from FOBB, I was able to monitor the disease closely. The best way to sum it up is that my husband felt, as we went through milestones that everyone else alongside us was going through as well, that if *he* went through milestones alongside everyone else, his life would turn into a bank commercial. There is something about finding yourself on what feels like a conveyor belt of homogeneous human experiences that's depressing and ennui-producing. (Ennui is the opposite of joie de vivre. Look it up.) It's even worse when that homogeneity is laid bare in an experience you thought was special.

Let me explain with a story from our pre-pregnancy days.

For our honeymoon, we went to a resort in Bora Bora. Because of the "gotta leave the day after the wedding" timing of honeymoons and the limited availability at the St. Regis Bora Bora, every single couple we talked to had been married the same day as us: October 12. Everywhere we went in the overpriced, corporate resort, there were other couples high-fiving over their love of breakfast buffets and October 12 weddings. We couldn't have felt less unique.

It didn't help that we were in a resort where everything was beige. Someone needs to tell all of the American luxury hotel chains that there's nothing magical about the color beige. Actually, it may be the best way to describe the sensation of finding yourself among a group of American tourists marching through the exact same life ritual as you: it feels "beige."

It feels very beige to realize that the most special event of your life—your individual confession of love before a group of your peers, the celebration of your commitment to sharing a life with another unique human being—happened at the exact same date and time as the blessed union of an investment banker and a tech headhunter who met at business school.

After the honeymoon, I had my own slight variation of FOBB: Fear of Being Beige. (The irony is that I look great in many shades of off-white: beige, ecru, mother-of-pearl. I can really pull off "muted.")

It's hard not to feel a little beige when you decide to have a baby. It really starts to feel like you are living the same life as every mother you meet. Especially when the first question a pregnant woman is likely to hear, particularly from other mothers, is: "What's your birth plan?"

A "birth plan" is a kind of battle strategy for the war between a fetus and your vagina. It's how you've decided to go about removing the kicking, undulating parasite that you will one day name Connor from your womb. Are you scheduling your cesarean section at the nearest hospital, which has every kind of blood on tap and a strategy to fight sepsis in case of an emergency, or are you having a water birth in the Black Sea? There are as many options as there are opinions on the wrong way to go about your baby's debut. Don't have vaginal birth? Your child will never feel loved and will be addled with allergies. Don't have a C-section? Your husband will never again feel the walls of your vagina and you'll be addled with infidelity.

Everything I read about pregnancy seemed horrifying. Did you know that if you only eat Cheetos your whole pregnancy, the baby will still get the nutrients it needs by sucking them from your body? It will feed off your bones, your tooth enamel, and your vitality. Isn't that called a parasite?

The idea of carrying and delivering a baby was terrifying to me. Gaining up to eighty pounds seemed annoying, especially at forty-two (albeit a remarkably svelte forty-two). I couldn't imagine going into stereotypical labor. In a hospital gown, screaming bloody murder, telling my husband to fuck off, grunting and moaning for up to thirty-six hours? It sounded like a horror movie, or at least a bad romantic comedy.

I couldn't picture my water breaking. My mom told me she was alone when hers broke, and I just had this idea that I would be casually going about my day when BAM! I'd lose control of my bowels, fall to the floor, and desperately try to wipe enough amniotic fluid off my fingers to get the Lyft app to load so I could get to the hospital. Once the app confirmed my "ambulance" (a 2001 Kia Sedona driven by Oscar—3.9 stars), I'd pick myself up off the floor of Costco's bulk toilet paper aisle, emitting terrifying yelps while employees started slipping on the growing puddle of crotch water. And then a pail of pig's blood would fall on me. (Not sure where the pig's blood was coming from, but that's how my vision always ended.)

"Natural childbirth" actually seemed impossible. I did not want to push. I also heard that Posh Spice scheduled her C-section, and the gossip magazines in England said she was "Too Posh to push." Never did anything ring truer. There was even an option to not carry the baby at all! "Too Posh to preg!" (This hasn't caught on, but I'm hoping this book will get it going.)

There are a lot of reasons people need surrogates, and I definitely tried to get my doctor to tell me I had one of them. "Do I maybe have a distended pelvic floor?" I asked him. He shook his head no. "Wouldn't a nineteen-year-old uterus be a better place for our child to be grown?" I mused. But no. He kept telling me again and again that my uterus was beautiful, gorgeous, a ten out of ten. I was starting to think he wanted to fuck my uterus. Honestly, I would have totally had a surrogate if I could have convinced my doctor to say I even sort of needed it. We even had an interview with a potential candidate, and it was only when she casually mentioned that she worked in a paint factory that I gave up on my plan. Fuck it, drop the egg in me, I'm not "too posh to preg" after all.

I guess I could picture going into labor. And I didn't like what I saw. I wanted to have a C-section.

If there's one thing I quickly learned from being pregnant, it's that I am NOT a hippie. Even though I don't trust the police, I smoke pot, and I have begrudgingly been to three out of seventeen Burning Mans, in my truest soul there lives a rich elderly Jewess from Manhattan's Upper East Side. I just want to be comfortable and pay you to make me feel no pain. Get the baby out safely, put me under if you have to, and wake me up when it's over. I prefer no forceps, but if you must use them, lovingly reshape the head and don't tell me what happened. I guess that was my birth plan.

Hippies have lots of advice. Approximately 100 percent of my friends extolled to me the wonders of eating their placenta, a practice now so widespread that the CDC had to issue a warning about placenta consumption. A woman in a moms' group I attended invited me over for plasagna. If you're going to cook something that comes out of your vagina, maybe don't make it a dish with layers of cheese? At the most I would vape my placenta.

Because literally everyone you talk to in LA is also an acupuncturist, it made sense that I was surrounded by people who frowned on the use of drugs to ease the pain of childbirth. It didn't matter that many of those people used plenty of recreational drugs in their real lives. When it came to childbirth, they wanted to feel the pain.

I knew a woman who wanted to give birth without drugs so badly that she CROSSED STATE LINES WITH HER DOULA to give birth in Nevada, because her baby was breech and the state of California won't deliver breech babies without an epidural. And in the shadows of John Ascuaga's Nugget Casino Resort, the crown jewel of Reno, she realized why.

It's fucking dangerous! After agonizing for eighteen hours, she was rushed in for an emergency C-section. If you don't know what that is, it's when you try to give birth naturally and it doesn't work and then the doctors frantically cut into your abdomen, often leaving a crooked scar, because their only priority at that moment is to get the baby out safely.

Naturally, I preferred a planned C-section. I had heard that they had outlawed vanity C-sections in Brazil because so many of the hot Brazilian women didn't want to blow out their vaginas and it was getting out of hand. Nobody had vaginal births there anymore. Fortunately, I wasn't planning on giving birth in Rio.

Three weeks before my due date, my doctor relayed the good news that the baby wasn't dropping, so I would most likely be "forced" to get a C-section. I asked if that meant we could schedule it. The doctor and I both looked in our calendars. I was free on my scheduled due date (minus an easily cancelable eyebrow wax), and he was too. I came back to the hospital on the appointed date at 9 a.m., I was in the operating room by 10, and the baby was plopped on my chest at 10:07. I still get compliments on my scar. A massage therapist once asked, "Ohhh, who did your C-section?"

Maybe a scheduled C-section is kind of beige. For me, being pregnant was the first time in my adult life I actually wanted to be a little beige, a little basic. Maybe not "my favorite thing to do on a Saturday night is order pad thai and watch *Friends* on Netflix" basic, but at least "let's put folic acid on my shopping list" basic. Even if you don't have a difficult pregnancy—and I was lucky not to—it's when your priorities start to shift. (At least for mothers; dads-to-be can do all sorts of things a mom-to-be can't—drink, smoke, not be called geriatric in their mid-thirties.)

There's a force far greater than the Fear of Being Basic or the Fear of Being Beige. It's the fear of doing something—anything— that could harm your child. It's the oldest fear there is (except for maybe being eaten by a dinosaur, which is really just a riff on the harm-your-child fear). The future of our species has basically always depended on mothers doing what's best for their babies, at least until the fathers have advanced far enough in their martial arts training to protect their offspring.

I think that's how pregnancy prepares you for parenthood. It teaches you how to be afraid. Before I was pregnant, when people told me I couldn't understand the love I'd have for my child, I didn't realize that meant I would be scared for the rest of my life that something would happen to it/her/them. That and I'd be worried for the rest of my days in a way that was all-consuming, bordering on crippling. Perhaps most mothers throughout history have felt this way, but I have to believe it's gotten worse in the era of the geriatric pregnancy.

Back in Pioneer Days, when people had twenty children, they had to know some were going to make it and some weren't. And you didn't have time to be sad: you had to get back to stacking hay or tending the hearth or eating out of metal bowls or whatever it is that people did back then.

When you're making one kid from one embryo with one frozen egg left over from the Obama administration, you don't have a huge margin of error. Pregnancy taught me to be afraid. I didn't know I was capable of so much fear. I mean love. Aren't those words basically interchangeable?

I once read that there are cultures that believe you aren't having children for this current life we live in but for five generations in the future. That always calmed my fears for a moment, until I remembered that the earth is on fire and the only people still around in five generations will be Elon Musk and his army of robots (See Chapter 10, Parenting in Environmental Panic).

We have plenty more chapters to discuss the fears, anxieties, and annoyances of being a mother. For now, I want to end the chapter with an important reminder to enjoy pregnancy. It can be hard, but as my friend and comedian Bonnie McFarlane once said, it's the last time people will feel obligated to be nice to you. And if all of the fear overwhelms you, just remember: there is a light at the end of the tunnel. Your death! (Or the death of our planet, whichever comes first.)

NOT PARTNERS

"People fall in love because they don't know each other yet."
—FRAN LEBOWITZ

*A*s much as I'm enjoying regaling my readers with tales of motherhood, I think we all might enjoy a chapter without any kid stuff in it, like the backseat of a wealthy childless couple's BMW.

And like the timeless story of rich yuppies whose German car's supple leather interior will never develop black mold because a toddler emptied six ounces of organic milk into the cupholder of the movable armrest and then nobody noticed for four months, this chapter is about partners. Not the partners we parent with, but the ones whose gene pools we were lucky enough to avoid.

Gene pools, after all, are like any other kind of pool: some have Moroccan tile mosaics on the bottom and are always heated to ninety-one degrees and will be loving and collaborative co-parents with you, and some are muddy holes. This chapter is about the muddy holes, the ones you swim in when you're hot and sweaty and young and inexperienced, when the water looks inviting and exciting but will just give you cold sores if you put your face in for too long.

"How do you expect me to look at that much liquid this early in the morning?!"

"I'm sorry, Christopher," I'd say, hanging my head for once again ruining my boyfriend's morning coffee by giving him slightly too much coffee.

"It's okay, Wiener," he would sigh. "Just don't let it happen again."

Then he would take a puff of his hand-rolled Drum cigarette and stare out the window, sulking at the injustice of his mug being filled too close to the top, and I would dump out a little coffee and bring it back to him, and he would eventually be nice to me again—until lunch, when we would have ANOTHER fight.

Side note: For years into my relationship with my husband, Moshe, whenever I'd pour him a cup of coffee he would stare at it, confused at how comically little coffee there was in the mug. I eventually healed from my PCSD (post-coffee stress disorder).

Our fights were frequent and covered a wide range of topics, all under the umbrella of me doing something incorrectly. Christopher would become angry, criticize me, and give me the silent treatment for such affronts as: the way I was walking; how wide I opened a window; if I gave him the wrong-sized knife to spread his marmalade; if I called marmalade "jelly" or, worse, jelly "jam"; or if I wasn't giving a Monet enough distance when I looked at it.

He claimed that his mother was "from" French aristocrats, which was why his standards were so high. I was "from" the Midwest, which he looked down upon, though he *did* say he thought his mother would have approved of my tiny ankles (essential for procreation, apparently, although I'm not sure any of us should be taking breeding advice from the incestuous nobility of Western Europe).

I was twenty-three and he was forty-one. I still can't believe the romance that this guy inspired in me. I remember buying up a bodega's worth of flowers and hauling them in three trips to the studio apartment in the East Village he had subletted for a week to be with me in New York. And this was before Instagram! My expensive and labor-intensive floral display had no chance of leading to a lucrative sponsored-post deal with 1-800-Flowers.

I would never do something so thirsty as that now, but I think I must've been, on some level, brainwashed, because I would have done anything for him. In fact, I did. I was so obsessed with Christopher that I eventually dropped out of college, gave up my rent-controlled apartment in Manhattan, sold all of my belongings, and moved to Australia for a year to pursue my new goal in life: making sure he woke up in a room full of flowers replete with tiny cups of coffee.

That's right: before I got married and had a kid, one of the most intense relationships I had was with a man who called me Wiener.

I was cocktail-waitressing in New York when we met. When he walked into my bar, our eyes locked. It was as if the world stopped around me. Today I would recognize his intense stare as that of a salivating psychotic zeroing in on his prey, but back then I thought it was destiny. I've since learned that if you enter a dissociative state when you make extended eye contact with a stranger, you might be in trouble.

I thought he was the height of sophistication. He looked like Mick Jagger in a vintage private school jacket. I soon learned this was his only cool jacket, but I was so sprung, I didn't care that he was usually wearing Bill Cosby sweaters. He was an intellectual-property lawyer who wrote book reviews for an Australian newspaper (I was a longtime subscriber) and had just returned from shooting a documentary about the first year of a festival in the desert called Burning Man, then and now an unfortunately integral part of my love life.

He was interested in how Burning Man connected to what he called "the information superhighway," which should tell you this relationship was a very, very long time ago, i.e., back when the internet was called the information superhighway. Pre-Facebook, pre-Instagram, pre–Tom from MySpace. Trump was some tacky guy from the eighties. Life was bliss! Until I got to Australia.

When I landed in Sydney, Christopher took me to our "love

shack." I walked in for the first time and my heart sank. It was a studio apartment with purple mesh hung up for curtains. It reminded me of a dorm room, with Ikea furniture in a corner. I fell asleep on a futon and woke up to the bass from the *Seinfeld* theme music.

I thought we would have tickets to the opera that night, but no such luck. He immediately started emotionally abusing me and, worse, all he seemed to want to do was watch John Candy movies, which he knew by heart.

As I saw him studying the want ads every morning, I asked, "What about your job as a book reviewer? Or your other job as a lawyer? Or your film, the one that's being funded?" He would get irate and tell me to mind my own business. Somehow, interactions like these made me fall deeper and deeper in love with him. (I told you, I was brainwashed.)

I cleaned his house, ironed his clothes (I feel you, Nana!), listened to his endless "gentleman-splaining" about any topic ever. And in return for all of that, he was controlling, critical, manipulative, and prone to creating public spectacles. He also had an inflatable-art collection. Sounds like a real catch, right?

There were many, many contradictions in him. Like he just seemed to sit around rewatching *Seinfeld* all day, but he would do it while eating an avocado with sour cream and caviar in the center. He acted like royalty, but we had to take the bus.

Once, in fact, we got on a bus and he called out to the driver as if we were in a Grey Poupon ad, "Excuse me, driver! Tell me, does this bus go to Bondi Beach?" "Read the sign," the bus driver retorted. Christopher stood up in a rage, flipped his scarf, and said, "Are you assuming, sir, that I can read?" (Among the royal set, there's no greater status symbol than functional illiteracy.)

He then demanded that the man stop the bus that instant, and he stormed off—with his wiener dog in tow. The bus driver, with a pity I was now starting to recognize, called after me, "Where'd ya meet that guy?"

He was completely dismissive and rude to anyone he thought was beneath him, which was everyone. Another time we were at a café, and when the waitress came to take our order he barely looked at her and whispered, "Croissant," like a seven-year-old Prince Charles giving his breakfast order to his morning nanny. When she returned with his croissant, he stood up and demanded, "What is this?! I wanted a bacon, egg, and cheese croissant!" She apologized and went to get him what he wanted. Having been a waitress most of my adult life, I told him that he'd been rude and he *had* only said, "Croissant," but he just seethed, whispering, "She knew what I meant!" like they were old enemies.

If we had to walk somewhere, he would always insist on walking in the direction that the winds were blowing the scent of flowers onto us. He would have no qualms about spending our (my) last $60 on a champagne picnic. We spent most of our time hiding in our pathetic love shack, however, because he hadn't yet mentioned me to his friends, all of whom I would later learn were just women he was fucking. The few times we did leave the house, I could tell that even strangers were worried about me. One time, a woman came up to us in a café. "Christopher! Your daughter is looking for you!" He quickly shooed her away from the table and said, "I have no children, Wiener. That woman is insane."

Why did I stay with someone so completely psycho as Christopher? I was a young idiot and I thought if someone said something, it was true. Plus he seemed to know about obscure records—until I learned he was just lying, which takes a lot longer when you don't have easy access to the information superhighway.

A lot of men I know become comedians so they can date out of their league. I wanted to date out of my social class, out of what I grew up with. I was like Meghan Markle, but way less lucky. (I couldn't even get an audition for *Suits*.)

In my head I was trash, and I wanted to know about wine, manners, art, fine dining, history, repartee, and luxury—you know, the American dream for a lady (that you find in Australia). Looking back, had I just gone to a fancy Manhattan prep school I could've bypassed this whole experience. This guy *appeared* to know it all. He knew so much about so much that I would sometimes fall asleep to his two-hour pontification sessions.

It's troubling to me to think that when I felt romance most intensely it was with someone who would've ruined my life if I had had a child with him. Thank goodness he left me for a girl in Brooklyn with an inheritance. By the grace of God, the universe, Allah, Jesus Christ, and instant karma, I escaped being impregnated by this person and allowed our relationship to be a meaningless blip in my life.

Imagine if that girl in Brooklyn's ankles had been a little more fat! I would've never finished college, found a career, met my great husband, had my gorgeous child, or written this book. Instead I'd be spending my miserable life protecting my child from getting tricked by their father into believing they're a member of the nonexistent Australian nobility.

Christopher offered me one thing: the promise of sophistication (if not the reality, although I'll concede that eating a caviar-stuffed avocado with a tiny spoon is strangely elegant). If I've learned one thing in my quest to find a partner, however, it's that one thing isn't enough. You need a list.

A therapist once urged me to write a list of what I wanted in a partner. I brought it to her the next week with items like "British" and "plays guitar." She said, "What about someone who cherishes you?" Hmmm, I had never thought of that. The closest I had was "isn't psycho" (thanks, Christopher!).

She said I should think about it a little more. She urged me to divide the qualities between "negotiable" and "nonnegotiable." Was it really a nonnegotiable for me to date someone who had a British accent? I would have to give up my lifelong dream of having my kid call his dad "Pa-*pa*" and calling potato chips "crisps," but who cares about a cute accent and crooked teeth if my partner treats me like garbage, or, as he might say, rubbish?

My list-making made me really zero in on what I wanted in a partner. I know some people get lucky and marry their high school sweetheart (my best friend, Lynn, did it), but I had to work at it. I had to keep meeting people, keep learning about myself, keep breaking up with people, keep getting broken up with, and keep adding to the list.

My list of nonnegotiables grew each time a relationship fell apart. I added new things I hadn't even known I wanted: "makes his own money," "lets me shine," "isn't jealous or controlling," "doesn't pour cocktails on my head in anger," "dog person."

I know what you're thinking: Is "dog person" really a nonnegotiable? Considering I sleep with three chihuahuas, "dog person" was kind of necessary. ("Not a cat person" was also on my list: I'm allergic to cats and I think having animal shit festering in a closet in your house is kinda gross. An English duke who played lead guitar could have a cat and I still wouldn't have dated him.)

Despite my experience with Christopher, "sophisticated" always remained on my list. When I first met my husband, Moshe, he brought over Ingmar Bergman's *The Seventh Seal*. If this sounds familiar, it's because Moshe and I share the same meet-cute first-date film as the greatest love story of our time, Woody and Soon-Yi.

I was very impressed with Moshe's choice. I couldn't believe he had such sophisticated taste. The fact that Moshe was into Bergman filled me with desire—but that was one of the last black-and-white films, art films, or Bergman films we ever watched. He was trying to impress me. It turns out our true tastes look more like this:

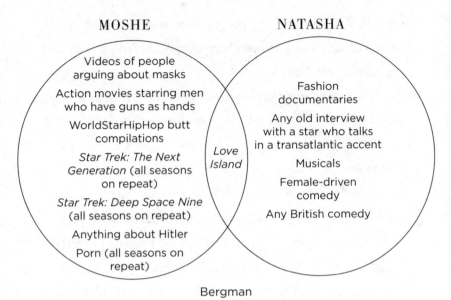

You might ask yourself, what could these two people possibly watch together? Without my influence, Moshe would watch every Marvel movie in a row and then start over; and left to my own devices, I would just go down a rabbit hole of obscure sixties musicals and interviews with the snobbiest artists of the last century. Since he can't make me watch *Star Trek* and I can't make him watch a four-hour conversation with Leonard Bernstein, we have to come up with something together as a couple that will stimulate us.

To our surprise, we both love documentaries, westerns, and Gordon Ramsay. And since Moshe is the only comedian I know who doesn't watch comedies, he came up with the idea that we watch the Best Picture winners from the beginning of the Oscars. This has been so much fun; we actually finished and are now on to the Best Screenplay winners. These are better movies on the whole than the Best Picture winners, but I highly recommend either of these projects. I'll watch all of the Best Costume winners on my own.

Here's what I learned in those years of dating: a partner should be fun to talk to, listen to you, and cherish and respect you, or should at the very least be a nice person you enjoy having sex with whose nickname for you isn't that of an actual dog.

Let's say you're lucky and you find someone who checks all those boxes, who has almost everything from your list. A person you can love even seven years and one pandemic later when you discover they clip their toenails in bed while drinking Funyuns dust from the bag and watching reruns of a *Star Trek* spin-off only truly dedicated nerds know about. (This is a hypothetical example and it's just a coincidence that my loving husband actually does all of these things.)

Congratulations, you've found your partner!

And then you decide to have kids with them.

I didn't have any family money, and I wanted to be in one of the hardest and most competitive professions that's ever existed. I'd seen my mom raising kids alone, not having help from family, not being able to finish college, not being able to do anything but work a menial job to pay for her kids, who were fathered by some-one she now hated. Just twenty-three, and all her joie de vivre gone.

My only chance was to make my own money first, then see

how I'd feel about kids. But I always knew that my maternal instincts probably wouldn't be ignited on their own. I would need to meet the right person first. I wanted a partner. Then *possibly* a child. I hadn't quite been convinced that the world deserved my children.

But when I met Moshe, right away he struck me as someone who could handle fatherhood. A man who didn't love me just for my ankles. And he wanted a kid. And he loved his family and he made me laugh and we fell in love and I deemed him worthy to fertilize one of my frozen eggs.

And that's when the real work began.

PARTNERS

"Diplomacy is the art of letting someone else have your way."
—DANIELE VARÈ

In every family, there's one parent who does more. Maybe it's a lot more, maybe it's a little more, and maybe, as in the case of some single parents, it's everything more. For the purposes of this chapter, the "mother" is that person who does more. And the "husband" is the person next to them, just a teensy bit worse at parenting than they are.

If you are two women in a relationship and you're wondering who the "mother" is, obviously you both are BUT . . . if you had major surgery or blew out your vagina to get the baby, you get to be the "mega mother," at least right at first.

I know this doesn't take gay men into account, so I'm proposing that the two fathers should have a pain contest and whoever can take the most pain can be the "mother." Maybe try sticking a tube up your urethra and seeing whose screams are the least blood-curdling? That's just one suggestion; I'm sure you guys could come up with your own feats of endurance.

Being a wife and mother is sometimes like being a waitress at a really shitty restaurant where the patrons don't tip and also sometimes leave their underwear on the floor. (Like the Denny's in my hometown.) I personally love my husband more and more with each passing sock he leaves on the dining room table, but studies show that many people love their partners less after childbirth.

It makes sense. With a new child in the mix, you're in a fertile environment for resentment, disagreement, and all sorts of drama. (Like the Denny's in my hometown.)

If you're a woman who has given birth, you've most likely been through hell. There's a high chance you had a C-section and a fairly high chance it was an "emergency," never a particularly comforting word to be associated with any major medical event and/or your reproductive organs. There are no good vagina emergencies. Men's penises, on the other hand, seem to be in a constant state of panic or near-panic.

Before the vagina emergency are countless mini emergencies: nausea, mood swings, weight gain, and vulnerability. And if you're like me, two years of fertility drugs prior to the pregnancy, i.e., injecting yourself in the butt every day until you force your husband to help because he has a "thing" about needles. And you have to deal with all of this in a state of relative sobriety, so all of your favorite coping mechanisms are off the table.

But then: you've got the baby. It's been removed from your stomach and set on your chest and now it's yours. You feel like a plane has crashed and you've made it to land. Besides your baby there's one other person who survived the crash. It's your partner—and they're wearing a VR headset and playing *Beat Saber* with a kid in Singapore.

In those early months, it's obvious the mom is running the show. Why? Because as long as you're nursing, you are the parenting overlord. How is someone supposed to disagree with your parenting philosophy when you are literally producing a dairy beverage from your tits that is the only thing keeping the child alive? Once your tits dry up, so does your power. You might need to actually listen to the rambling nonsense your husband has to say about "his child." Maybe this is why some mothers keep nursing until their child gets pubic hair?

My husband and I share a worldview—it's a big part of why we got married, of course—but the disagreements about the child started immediately. Our first fight was over getting a surrogate. I don't know why, but I was extremely afraid of being pregnant. It just struck me as something that modern technology could take care of, like Amazon Prime for my uterus.

I saw nothing beautiful in pregnancy. Imagining myself pregnant meant imagining myself as a bloated mammal in the wild. It seemed like I would be hosting a growing cyst (a cyst I now love deeply) inside me and it might destroy my body forever. I was excited about being a mom but I didn't understand why in order to become a mother, I had to potentially ruin my body. This is an extremely vain outlook and I'm not proud of it (or at least feel like I have to say I'm not), but it's how I felt.

After our meeting at the surrogacy agency, my husband told me he felt really uncomfortable with the whole thing. He said it was weird to rent out a person's body to house our baby. I argued that the woman wanted to do it, it was good money for her, and since I wouldn't have to become a bloated hippie, I could still work to pay for it. He won. "Okay, fine," I said. "I'll carry your baby, but you owe me."

I might have kept the last part to myself, but we didn't Airbnb another woman's womb, and by some miracle our last embryo took and I got pregnant. I had made peace with carrying the baby and I figured now my husband and I could go back to agreeing on everything.

And then it was time to think of names.

Just because you and your partner hate all of the same people doesn't mean you will agree on a baby name. Our second big fight was that my husband really wanted the baby to have a Jewish name. I'm a proud Jew-by-choice, but a lot of Jewish names don't quite have a ring to them. Names like Dudu, Schlema, and Harvey Weinstein.

My husband was exclusively pitching Jewish names. One in particular he would keep bringing up is Tikva. I explained to him I wasn't naming my daughter something that sounds like a disease that farm animals get: "We had to put the mare down, she had tikva."

The name means "hope" in Hebrew, and Hope was his grandmother's name. While I think that is a beautiful gesture, there is no way in hell I'm carrying this thing AND going to call it a name the kid will have to repeat 100 percent of the time when she is introducing herself. I would constantly replay in my head Li'l Tikva's first day on the schoolyard:

"Hi, I'm Tikva."

"Teekba?"

"Tikva."

"Tickbug?"

"Tikva."

"TikTok?"

That is something I wouldn't wish on anyone. (Apologies to all the actual Tikvas out there. I'm sure many of you are wonderful people.)

My husband is half Jewish, half hippie, so when he wasn't suggesting hard-to-pronounce Hebrew names, he was tossing out hippie names. There was a solid month he wanted her to be named Coconut. I feel like "Coconut Kasher" might have limited prospects in the job world. What if she wanted to be a Supreme Court justice, or even just a TV judge? No one is taking the rulings of Judge Coconut seriously, even if they're delivered on a set that shares a sound stage with infomercials for blenders that can also grill meat.

(On the flip side, giving our daughter a Jewish name would almost guarantee she never became a stripper. Nobody has ever said, "Clapping her pussy in the champagne room, give it up for Brindle!")

My husband's name—Moshe, which is somehow an even more Jewish version of Moses, which is literally the most Jewish name in recorded human history—is mispronounced 70 percent of the time, and I think he thinks that's cool because it's unique. Well, except in the Torah.

I have a name that is unique but never mispronounced, and that's what I wanted for my child. Finally, after much searching, the name we settled on was Jewish, easy to pronounce, unique, and cosmopolitan, and if I tell you what it is, you might steal it and then my child might grow up like a Jennifer. Which would be worse than Tikva. (*Not* sorry to all the actual Jennifers out there. Your parents were *real* basic.)

But the disagreements didn't stop there.

My husband and I both agree with everything that Bernie Sanders says, but can't seem to agree on the correct way to fasten the baby's diaper. Or how to get her into a car seat. Or how much time she should spend in the sun without a hat. Or if she's ready to start using a spoon to eat. Or how long to put a phone in front of her face. We share core values but disagree about minutiae. And parenting is minutiae. Two parents can agree on how to live but have very different ideas on the best way to keep a child alive.

I've always known that my husband and I were different from each other. I've never been told to calm down by a flight attendant. I've never gotten into a screaming match with a Lyft driver. My husband, on the other hand, enjoys nothing more than a good argument with a complete stranger.

For example, one night we were celebrating his mom's birthday at a cute restaurant near our house. It's the kind of place that's been around since the 1920s and serves prime rib and has caroling in the winter. Our baby had eaten (she loves traditional cuts of meat) and wanted to walk around the restaurant holding my hand. I would say she was being a 3 on the annoying scale, 10 being your classic meltdown on an airplane.

All of a sudden, Moshe heard a man three tables over complaining loudly to the manager that our kid was running around the restaurant. At which point Moshe announced across the dining room, "If you have something to say to me, say it to my face!" Thus began a screaming match over the three white-tableclothed tables separating us. The man said, "You shouldn't take your child to nice restaurants!" Moshe retorted, "If you think this is a nice restaurant, you need to get out more, homie!"

I know my husband is activated back to the street persona of his youth when he starts using words like "homie." I call this persona "Old Moshe" because it seems like a remnant of his days as a teen dropout in Oakland. You don't want to argue with Old Moshe, because he's a gifted orator who doesn't lose arguments, and you don't know what he's stashing in the giant hems of his hood-hippie jeans.

The man at the restaurant stood up and yelled, "You have your kid running around the restaurant like this is Disneyland!" Moshe smiled, delighted by what he had heard. He pointed to a gold plaque hanging right above a booth; it read WALT DISNEY'S TABLE. Moshe shouted, "This was *literally* Walt Disney's favorite restaurant!" The entire restaurant, which had wisely been staying out of this dispute between two adult men, burst into laughter.

I tell this story not to tout my husband's unmatched debating skills and excellent crowd work, but as an illustration of behavior I would never exhibit. I would never start shouting in a restaurant unless there was extreme danger or a waiter wore a button that read "Free bottle of Pinot for the loudest scream!"

These differences have played out in various and, let's say, more annoying ways since we had a child. You see, my husband is reckless and I am paranoid. Or if you are trying to be generous, he is adventurous and I am careful. Or as I like to think of it, he is a maniac and I am normal.

We took our daughter camping recently—a sentence I never thought I'd write—and got into a fight because he wanted her to enjoy the campfire from her nylon, made-in-a-sweatshop, probably highly flammable pack 'n play just a little too close to the fire for my taste. So I would move it back a couple inches. He would move it toward the fire. I would move it back, and then we would get into a fight.

You've made the most important decision of your life with someone, and now you have to agree with them on all these other decisions. Like, do we need to start smelling burning hair before we move the baby away from the campfire?

A child is a lot of work. And even with division of labor, one member of the family is just going to absorb more of that work.

Kids make a mess. A mess needs to be cleaned up, so you and your partner are now professional cleaners. Or one of you is. Or you live in unorganized chaos where you can't find the caps to anything in the fridge. It often feels like the contents of a junk drawer have been emptied every few feet across my home. If you have any aesthetic sense, you would think our house is a mess. Moshe was raised by an ex-hoarder, so he walks in the front door, steps over a scattered pile of tools I didn't know we had but my daughter somehow found and threw all over the floor, and thinks we're nailing it.

And when you go on vacation, it's even more work. It's not a vacation with a baby, it's paying money to do chores in a pretty location. When our child was a year and a half old, we went to Mexico for my husband's birthday. (My husband might be the first Jew to pick up surfing at thirty-seven.)

Our daughter always slept through the night, so we didn't anticipate any fussing from her. Our first night in the hotel she screamed for six hours, wouldn't sleep in her crib, and wouldn't respond to any of our efforts with anything less than a resort-rattling wail. I knew she wasn't hungry because I had made a frantic peanut butter sandwich in the bathroom and tried to toss it into her mouth in tiny pieces as she howled. She was crying so loudly that my husband and I could barely hear ourselves arguing about what to do next with her. (Me: Go back to America and rush to the ER. Him: Brush her teeth again.)

We moved from one scream-inducing activity to the next. We pulled out every toy, turned on the AC, turned off the AC, sang to her, offered water, gave Tylenol. The night is mostly a blur, but I do remember waking up alone shivering on a bare bed with a hand towel as a blanket and my husband on the tile floor in the corner, also shaking, wrapped in the sheets that had been on the bed with the baby in his arms. She was finally snoring. There are only two things that could get you to wake up like that: a baby or heroin.

The young, childless woman who was running the hotel said that when she walked into the room the next morning, she had "never seen anything like it." Granted, there was an upside-down spatula sticking out of a peanut butter jar on the toilet, but still a rude comment.

Back at home, I'm lucky that I'm able to hire people to help me, because I think if our nanny worked even one less hour a week, I would get a divorce. The idea of being a mother didn't really appeal to me until I was forty, so I hadn't spent any time thinking about what it entailed. I am fortunate enough to delegate some of the more unpleasant responsibilities to professionals, so my husband and I are left with the good stuff, like hiding in the bedroom and watching *Love Island* while the nanny tells our daughter within earshot of our bedroom door that "Mommy and Daddy are working." She's right: decompressing *is* working!

I know we have it good. If my husband and I were fighting over whose turn it was to clean out the Diaper Genie, I would've left him for my meditation teacher by now. But even with all the help that residuals from *Comedy Central Roasts* can pay for, there's still work to be done.

No relationships are exactly fifty-fifty. I am married to a man who I always think seven steps ahead of. I've already changed the diaper, made coffee, fed the baby, fed three different dogs three different dog foods, and put the baby in a smart little Yves Saint Laurent jumper while my husband is still in bed, finishing up a "wake-up argument" with an out-of-state teenager on Facebook about the meaning of *antifa*.

I think time is shaped differently for men. If my husband is with the baby for forty-five minutes, he's ready for some R and R at the Korean spa. I feel like every time I ask him to watch the baby, within five minutes he's screaming, "HONEY? Where do we keep the_____?" (Insert obvious thing that any functioning member of a household would know where to find.)

But I tried to see what my husband was bringing to the table, and as time went on it started blowing my mind to realize there are things he is actually good at. He does 100 percent of the cooking (beyond my specialty, "toast and coffee") and can whip up amazing vegan cookies or the world's greatest salad dressing from whatever he finds in the cabinet. He also knows the meaning of almost every word in the dictionary and is up-to-date on every current news story. I'd much rather talk to him for five minutes than google "what's up with Brexit." Oh, AND he thinks driving is fun.

The point is: I love my husband. But as time goes on, you can start to feel less like lovers and more like partners in a failing small business. It's like you and your partner own a Kinko's franchise and are just trying to keep the lights on.

How do you transcend parenthood to get back to your relationship? Because after all the talk about snacks, diapers, and whose turn it is to carry the wet wipes, don't forget: soon you will have to fuck this person! There's a reason the co-managers of Kinko's don't fuck. At least, not at well-run Kinko's.

I've tried to find a time to have sex that works for me. My husband wants to fuck at two in the morning after I've already fallen asleep to a nature documentary. I like to have sex when I'm fully awake. But since I've made a commitment to try to fuck my husband once a week, I've decided it's okay to have sex during my child's nap.

(If you're co-sleeping with your child, you might as well wear a loose-fitting pajama shirt that says *I Don't Fuck My Husband Anymore.*)

Your spontaneity in your relationship will be affected by children, and finding time for your partner will be a challenge. My therapist told me about a book called *The 5 Love Languages*, by Dr. Gary Chapman, which helped me. The book says there are five ways to show someone you love them: Words of Affirmation, Quality Time, Receiving Gifts, Acts of Service, and Fucking. (Dr. Chapman calls this Physical Touch, but we know what he means.)

Taking Dr. Chapman's online quiz helped me realize that I need more presents from my partner. And that my main love language is Acts of Service—that's how I show love and that's what I want from a lover in order to feel loved. Often the one that people use is the one they need. My husband is always telling me he loves me, so I've tried to start telling him more how I feel about him and I can tell he likes it. I try to do it right before I ask him to pick up his socks, or to please not leave his sweaty boxing wraps draped across my bathroom.

As hard as things can get, you and your partner always need to remember that you have the same ultimate goal: to raise a human being who will one day return the favor and wipe your ass when you get old. Oh, and hopefully likes you.

HELP! (FREE AND PAID)

"No hot nannies."
—CHRISSY TEIGEN

I didn't grow up with a nanny. I figured they were all like Rebecca De Mornay in *The Hand That Rocks the Cradle*: a hot blonde who would move into my house, seduce my husband, and eventually murder me. My friend grew up with a nanny, and he told me that when he was five, his nanny whispered to him, "I'm your real mom."

I went to day care and it was a less-than-magical place. It felt like juvenile hall but with toys. I don't remember much from this time period, just that I hated day care, with its fluorescent lighting, watered-down grape juice, and bulk containers of stale Goldfish crackers. Not having to go to day care was my loftiest dream; I longed for a time when I could jaunt home after school and settle in for some extremely unsupervised TV watching.

I was born in 1974, two years after the legalization of birth control for unmarried women. Until then, contraception was seen as "obscene, lewd, and lascivious." An unmarried woman with a diaphragm in her purse might as well have been a black-market distributor of Scandinavian horse porn.

Without birth control pills, women would have just continued to have sex, get pregnant, and then stay at home with the kids, i.e., never accomplish their dreams. Sadly for my mom, she was a member of the last generation of women who still thought they had to start a family with the first guy they met at the beach.

Unfortunately for her, as first guys you meet on the beach often do, my dad left her soon after she popped out three kids. She could have used some help. She worked a job and raised three kids on her own, one of whom had serious behavioral issues. The only help she had available to her was at the Catholic school, which was often highly suspect. I remember being in elementary school and standing in line to hand our teachers a slip, signed by our parents, that gave the principal permission to hit us. My mom, single and clueless about how to discipline us, was the only parent to sign. If I were a single mom of three, one of whom was "difficult," I'd be tempted to let a monsignor thwack my kids now and then in the hopes it would exorcise their demons. (For the record, I was never slapped.) Times change. Instead of requesting permission to rough up your kid whenever the mood strikes, schools now ask if it's safe for them to be in the same building as a bag of almonds.

After school, if we weren't staying late so the principal could whack us with a paddle embossed with the official crest of our Catholic school, we would go to day care.

Finally, when I turned thirteen, my dream came true. I became a latchkey kid, which I think is just what they used to call kids with working parents so it didn't seem illegal to leave us home alone until 7 p.m. Every day I would come home from school, count my notes from my friends (this is how we communicated before iPhones), wrestle off my tight stone-washed jeans, make some instant mashed potatoes, and settle in for an episode of *Gilligan's Island*. Heaven.

To be clear, the SS *Minnow* wasn't my first choice for entertainment. I was a victim of Tipper Gore's backlash. For those who might not remember her, Tipper Gore was married to then-senator, later-vice-president, even-later-should-have-been-president-but-for-the-stupid-Supreme-Court Al Gore, and she was very against the lack of wholesomeness in American entertainment.

Tipper Gore is the one who got the words *PARENTAL ADVISORY: EXPLICIT CONTENT* on CDs (this is how we listened to music before iPhones). She also took 2 Live Crew to court and won a great victory for morality, forcing them to change the lyrics in one song from "pop that pussy" to "pop that coochie." And that's why to this day your pastor still calls them "coochies."

My mom heard about Tipper's court battle and decided our family should boycott MTV. She found a company that put a padlock on the cable box so we couldn't have access to the station. I eventually learned how to pick the lock, but for at least a year, unable to watch my beloved *Yo! MTV Raps* or *120 Minutes*, I was forced to watch Nick at Night like some Quaker tween.

Every afternoon I would sit in front of the TV with my mashed potatoes (I told you I was great at microwaving dehydrated foods) and watch reruns of old sitcoms like *Gilligan's Island*, *The Mary Tyler Moore Show*, and *Green Acres* while I "babysat" my younger brothers. Perhaps it was from these shows that I learned comedic timing, so I guess I have Tipper Gore to thank for my sitcom career.

So the TV raised me, but now I'm trying to focus on raising my child without so much screen time. And now I realize why my mom let me watch so much TV. There's never time to do anything. I'm used to multitasking, doing everything on my own. (I'm what they call in show business a "multihyphenate": writer–performer–international style icon.) I resented having to ask my husband to bring me a glass of water so I could stay hydrated while the baby gnawed on my breast. I thrive in a clean environment. Once I had a baby, keeping the house clean turned into a pipe dream. I'm in a good mood when my house is spotless, when there's not popcorn detritus all over the sheets or used socks on the dining room table or a half-eaten box of animal crackers in a plant. And those are just my husband's messes. I need help.

My mom was retired by the time I had my daughter. Why couldn't she spend her first free time in more than forty years offering me the type of extra help with my child that she didn't have with her own? Isn't this what grandparents are for? Aren't grand-parents the greatest source of free labor since the unpaid Holly-wood internship? And you don't even have to read their pilot script to make up for helping them to "break into the industry."

If only it were that simple.

One drawback to having kids late is that by the time you get around to replicating your genetic material, your parents have de-volved into these people who you don't want touching your baby without supervision for fear that their artificial hip might slip out of alignment and your baby will come crashing down, or that the iPad they were staring at instead of watching your child will slip out of their arthritic fingers and blind your kid.

It's not their fault. No one really knows how to be a grand-parent. And it's got to be scary for them too.

It's a mystery until your child is born which of your parents is going to be good with your kid. All of the grandparents in my family have something wrong with them. My mom can only see out of one eye, my husband's mother is deaf and has no equilib-rium, and, most concerning of all, my father is Italian.

My mom has decided she will connect with my child primar-ily through sending her presents from the Woodfield Mall in Illi-nois. Clothes, gloves, hats, swimsuits, cookies, books, tomatoes from her garden. There are packages coming constantly—and like many older people, she is obsessed with what time the packages are arriving. There are always forwards from USPS with tracking numbers, times, signatures needed, and pleas for me to be home at

3:11 because that is when the package requiring a signature will arrive. I keep telling my mom that my child has more toys and clothes and hand-me-downs than we know what to do with, but that doesn't stop her from sending moccasins in four colors. I guess because my mother lives far away, buying my child things she doesn't need must bring her great joy. But we are past the time period when a package is exciting. Amazon took that from us. And my mother, forever scared that something will go wrong, double- and triple-tapes all her packages so you have to look for tools (razor blades, a table saw, a TIG welder) to even open them. I would rather she spend the money on a plane ticket and see my kid so they can have a relationship without the United States Postal Service acting as a middleman, but until she gets more adventurous, I'll continue to get paper cuts opening her packages and my child will look cute in her new bowler hat from "Grammy."

Then there are the mothers who aren't related to you. Your in-laws.

As much as I had hoped I would marry into New England money, I married into deaf hippies. I really had my eye on a summer house in Martha's Vineyard that I could escape to if there is ever another infectious disease, or at the very least, I'd get invited to drunk clambakes in the summer. But no such luck. Leave it to me to marry into the only family of camping Jews. My husband's family loves camping. I am not a camper. In fact, my favorite thing in the world, besides sleeping in my bed, is sleeping in someone else's bed in a luxury hotel. So when I see my husband late at night scrolling RVs for sale, I get nervous. We already have two, although I've laid down the law that our yard has a one-RV maximum. The other one is parked at his family's cabin that his grandfather built. I also didn't know Jews built cabins.

My husband always wants to hang out with his mom. That's the one thing that's always struck me about his family. They seem to . . . I don't know . . . enjoy spending time together? I know, it's weird. They get together whenever they can. As soon as I had the baby, his mom, stepdad, and brother all moved within several blocks of us. I know, you're jealous. Sometimes they will all be gathered in a room by the fire, all on their digital devices, just silently enjoying each other's company. Is this insanity better than clambakes on the glorious seascapes of the Northeast?

My husband's mother always says what she means and is a very positive person. Despite this kind of alien behavior, I do cherish the opportunity to study what it is about her that her children love so much, so that I can emulate it and my child will always want to be around me.

That's not to say she's a perfect or even "safe" choice for childcare. I once had to remind her not to give the baby SlimFast. It isn't the most dangerous beverage to feed a baby—apart from causing minor dehydration and containing sugar alcohols that are not easily absorbed by the small intestine—but it's not the typical one-year-old's drink of choice. On the bright side, I'm glad my child was already learning the importance of staying thin.

My husband's stepfather is great but has never had children of his own and is a bookish, cerebral entomologist, more likely to teach my child about pesticide alternatives in the California aphid population than to sing her "Ladybugs' Picnic."

My dad is like a character out of *Goodfellas*. Well, more like a character at a *Goodfellas* cosplay convention. For fun he drives around in his Thunderbird (yes, of course he calls it "The T-Bird") with the vanity license plate (JLEGGS—short for his nickname Johnny Leggs), with the seat all the way back like a gangster so you can barely see the top of his head, and he honks at the other Italians driving by. He's always name-dropping random Italians like they are names on the guest list at the Met Ball. Louie Bologna, Donny Salami, Carmine Cornish Game Hen. Most of his friends are named after meat.

And, like most Italians, my father is obsessed with meat. My husband and I have told him many times we don't eat red meat, yet every time he comes to visit he confusedly asks, "Not even venison?" Like we might make an exception for deer. He doesn't understand why we don't keep cured ham in the house, because "prosciutto isn't red, it's pink." Whenever my dad comes to visit, the refrigerator stinks of roast beef, pepperoncinis, and nine different cheeses. "The Italians are in town!" my husband will say when he opens the fridge.

My dad is a used-car dealer who has never been in the mob— but for some reason he acts like Al Capone whenever he's at a restaurant. Every time he orders something, he calls the waiter over with his pinkie ring (he has more pinkie rings than pinkies):

"Hey, sweetheart, what did I tell you? Does that look like *light* ice? I said a Dewars with *light ice*. I want to taste the alcohol. If I wanted to taste water, I'd stick a garden hose in my mouth."

Or, "How am I supposed to eat this pasta with all this sauce?" He turns to me, displaying the very reasonably sauced plate of pasta. "Tell me that's not a lot of sauce. I want to taste the pasta. If I wanted to taste sauce, I'd stick a bottle of Ragú in my mouth." He always has a helpful alternative for what he could be tasting instead of what he's being served. And it works! I guess at a restaurant people will remake your food and drinks for you. I know my mom didn't want to keep doing it.

My father also truly believes he's going to win the lottery. He plays scratchers every day and has a desk at his house dedicated exclusively to his lottery "work." In forty years of playing the lottery, the only thing he has ever won was two free tickets to play the lottery. And those two tickets . . . did not win the lottery! The last time I was home I asked him, "Don't you think the Lotto is a scam and a waste of time and money?" Sitting at his special Lotto desk, bits of papers spread out everywhere, he pulled his glasses down to his nose and looked me directly in the eyes and whispered, "I *will* win." To be honest, he was so sincere, I kind of believed him.

He visited us in LA recently, and I happened to FaceTime him as he was walking across a dangerous bridge with my child to get to a 7-Eleven to, you guessed it, play Lotto. I was so upset that I started crying uncontrollably at work and begged him to wait there until I could come get them both. I knew deep down my daughter was probably fine, but my dad doesn't know the city, it was a narrow bridge with a walkway that goes against traffic, and he can barely walk because like all Italians who eat only meat, my father has gout.

But that's not why I cried. Not really. The thing that made me start bawling at work was the thudding realization that as hard as I try, if I'm not there (heck, even if I am), I still can't protect my child from everything. That is a very heavy thought when "You've never loved anything like this and you cannot protect them" starts kicking in. I can protect my child as fiercely as humanly possible, but someone related to me can still take her on a narrow bridge against traffic to place a state-sponsored gambling bet.

So I can't rely on the grandparents and I can't rely on my husband and I can't rely on myself, so what to do? I started looking into nannies. Not too long ago, I saw a viral post from a Silicon Valley CEO who was looking for a nanny who could ski, drive in foreign countries, coordinate overseas holidays, cook vegan meals, and, perhaps most important, be comfortable river-swimming. This post played into everything I thought I knew about nannies—or really, the parents who hired nannies—they seemed bad.

But I needed help.

There are a lot of hard parts about being a mother, but asking for help might be the hardest. Or at least the second-hardest, after the ejection of a living creature from your abdomen.

The truth is: talking about hiring someone to help raise your child is a really uncomfortable subject. Even among mothers, it's hard to talk about. Every choice one mother makes, makes another mother feel judged. For every type of mother, there's another mother shaming her choices on Facebook. Personally, I judge any mother who's on Facebook in the first place.

It turns out the only thing harder than asking *for* help is asking *about* help.

One of the major benefits of waiting two decades beyond normal childbearing age to become a parent is that by the time you have the kid, you might have enough money to pay someone to help you raise it. So if you're very lucky, and can afford it, there are many amazing women out there who earn a living helping losers like you. They're called nannies, and they don't all look like Rebecca De Mornay. (Although, as we will soon discuss, some do.)

Like I said, when I was a child, my nanny was the TV set, and I grew up to be one of America's foremost tastemakers. Did I really need one for my child? According to my actress friends, absolutely.

"Get a night nurse" is the first thing any fellow actor or actress says to you when you're pregnant. Like it's this secret code. One friend recommended I take out a loan to afford it. "It's worth it," he said. I started to wonder if these people even wanted to be around their kids. Even though it seemed extremely crazy to me to have a stranger sleeping in the room with my new baby, I thought I had to figure out how to make this work financially. After all, if the third lead on a non-streaming cable show was suggesting it, how could it be wrong?

Night nurses cost about $10 to $20 MORE an hour than a regular nanny, and I had to beg my husband to be on board. I justified that it would help us sleep so we could be more productive in the day, thus making more money to pay for it. I interviewed many night nurses, one of whom came with a photo album of her nannying various celebrities' children. As my husband and I perused the swimsuit shots of her and some forgettable action star's children playing at a beach by some rock, I realized that this didn't feel like something I wanted. But I didn't know what I was doing, and, against my better judgment, I went for it.

I finally settled on a woman from Bulgaria who'd just come off a night nurse job with a friend. Everyone told us to have a night nurse start the first day we were home with the baby, so within a few hours of returning from the hospital after my three-day stay, the doorbell rang. To say we weren't in the mood for visitors would be an understatement. Realizing that having a stranger at our home during this insane adjustment period would be crazy, we'd tried to text her when we got home from the hospital to start the next day, but she never got the text. In fact, I'm not positive she'd ever gotten a text. In fact, I'm not positive she knew what texts were. In fact, I'm not positive she didn't communicate mainly by notes tied to a falcon's talon back in the old country. We later learned that, like many aged foreigners, she only communicated through WhatsApp (warning sign!).

So our first night home from the hospital there was a strange woman muddling bulgur wheat (I'm guessing?) in the nursery with our baby while my husband and I whispered to each other in our room next door. At 6 p.m., I told him to go get the baby and bring her to me for a feeding. He knocked at the nursery door and a gruff voice, hardened by whiskey shots shared with comrades at a checkpoint during the Cold War (I'm guessing) barked, "Don't knock! Just come in." My husband apologized and then asked if he could take the baby. She nodded: "Yes, it is allowed." At 9 p.m., she was supposed to meet me in the hallway with my baby so I could breastfeed. I went into the hallway, no nurse. I finally walked into the nursery, and she was sleeping. Hard, snore-filled Bulgarian sleeping. I mean, I get that they are going to sleep, but maybe not day one, first task. I woke her and the baby, breastfed them both, and went back to hiding in my room. My husband and I took to tiptoeing around our own home and wondering when we were allowed to see our baby. This didn't seem tenable.

The breaking point came around midnight when my husband opened the nursery door and the woman was standing over our child, in pitch dark, staring at it. (Possibly to make up for being asleep for her first task?) He shut the door, ran into our room, and said that he thought she was casting a spell on her. Needless to say, that was the only night we had her. It still cost us a small fortune, as I paid her for three weeks of work anyway; that seemed like the right thing to do because, even if she was a witch, she'd cleared her schedule for us.

I didn't need a night nurse. I was having to get up and pump anyway, so a stranger bringing me my baby in the hallway was a luxury I did not need. Walking myself into her bedroom just felt easier. What wasn't easy was trying to clean after major abdominal surgery, trying to become a mother, trying to cook for the first time, scheduling my life around breastfeeding and pumping, cleaning up after my husband, doing laundry, and doing the baby's laundry with a special detergent. I was overwhelmed and drowning. I *really* needed a nanny. Or a wife.

Once you've decided to hire a nanny, how do you find one?

In Los Angeles, many nannies fall into one of two categories. There are the younger women, the "cool aunts" who are trying to get their SAG card and don't help around the house. They don't have kids of their own, but they do have a highlight reel you can watch.

And then there are the older women, or the "young grandmas" (or "young gan-gans," if they're British, though you'll definitely pay a Doubtfire-level premium for that), who are probably better at cooking, cleaning, and child-rearing than you are, because they've already done it.

There's actually a third option: the au pair. Even the name sounds sexy. If hiring a nanny was up to the man, I'm sure we would all have a young Argentinian with a sexy accent in thigh-high boots taking care of the kids. It's hard enough for most men to get through the day without masturbating. The last thing your husband needs is a twenty-two-year-old aspiring musician sleeping right next to the room he showers in, tempting him to drill a Porky's-sized hole into their shared wall.

Why would anyone get a hot nanny? Even if *you* don't think

she's that hot, your husband probably does. Ben Affleck fucked the nanny. So did Arnold Schwarzenegger, effectively *terminating* his marriage to a Kennedy. Gwen Stefani's husband did it too. If you look up a picture of Gwen Stefani's old nanny, she looks exactly like Gwen did when she was starting out. If I were Sienna Miller, I would have a very hard time believing my husband would find anyone hotter than me. But alas, while she was off shooting a movie, her husband decided to start an affair with the young, not-as-attractive-as-Sienna nanny she hired to take care of everything while she was gone.

So how does this happen? Why do people do it? Is it a status thing to hire a nanny who appears to be your cool friend?

There's actually a service in LA called Educated Nannies. It's hard to imagine a more offensive business name. It's like calling a law firm Honest Jews.

Whether you hire an older woman with four kids of her own or an aspiring Instagram influencer who looks like your younger sister trying to make it on Broadway, one thing is certain: it's stressful figuring out who will help you take care of your kid. But that's just the beginning. The relationship with your child's nanny is one of the most intimate relationships that you can have as a new mom.

I was looking for someone to help me with the towering dishes, sterilizing the bottles, and watching the baby so I could recover from my C-section. I got very lucky that my friend had just finished needing the services of a woman who had four kids in college and years of experience as a nanny. For a year and a half she helped me with all things baby, not to mention cooking delicious soups, helping me clean up after my husband, cleaning up after me, and in general lovingly entertaining my daughter so I didn't have to put her in front of YouTube all day. And she never once cornered me about her improv career.

Maybe I'm a completely undomestic person, but without another woman helping me in my home, I don't think I could have accomplished what I've accomplished since having the baby without falling into a deep depression. I wouldn't be able to microwave the food, do the shopping, do the laundry, do the dishes—and still do my job.

There are days when I want nothing more than to share every waking moment with my daughter. There are other days when spending a full day with a baby feels like the worst job I've ever had. And I've done stand-up in Reno. A lot of the time, after I've spent eight hours with a toddler, my kid is definitely getting the worst of me. Exhausted, I once let her eat just syrup for dinner.

I was nervous about getting a nanny, but if you find the right one, it can actually be beautiful; I mean there's a third person in the house who loves your child. They allow them to experience love while you experience another episode of *Emily in Paris*. Is this lazy? Is this abdicating your responsibility as a parent? Perhaps. But you deserve a break sometimes. Feel no guilt and let someone else help (that's a Bulgarian saying).

And if it's a fantasy that you could afford to hire a nanny while you're at work, there's always day care. I went to day care, and look, you're reading my book right now.

DISCIPLINE

"Do not handicap your children by making their lives easy."
—ROBERT A. HEINLEIN

Growing up with an overwhelmed single mother, I was disciplined in many ways that were big in the 1980s. Throughout most of my childhood, I was pretty obnoxious and tended to say whatever popped into my head—sort of like a male comedian.

Unlike a male comedian, however, I was often punished for "telling it like it is" and "just saying what everyone is thinking." My mother's favorite punishment was sentences. I don't mean like being sentenced to a week without TV or a Saturday night in my room. I mean like actual sentences, with words. You know the opening credits of *The Simpsons*, where Bart Simpson writes sentences on a chalkboard? Like that.

My mother would have me go into my room and write "I will not disrespect my mother" a thousand times. I was punished with sentences so often that I'd carry my notepad with me to school on the bus, just to keep from falling too far behind and having to write new sentences about how I didn't finish my sentences. So I was always "finishing my sentences."

Before too long I realized that, (1) The quickest way to finish my sentences was to write "I, I, I, I, I, I" vertically down the entire page, then "will, will, will, will, will," etc., and, (2) There was no way my mom was counting to see if I did a thousand.

In retrospect, it was kind of soothing in a Zen way and probably explains why I have such great penmanship. But the hundreds of thousands of sentences I was made to write regarding my big mouth did not effectively shrink it, and today I make a good living disrespecting my mother in front of crowds—like any comedian, male or female.

My mother trafficked in other Reagan-era discipline hits. When I swore, for example, my mouth was washed out with soap, which was so gross it kind of worked, at least for as long as my tongue was being scrubbed. Do you know how hard it is to say "motherfucker" with a bar of Zest between your teeth?

For the worst infractions, we had a big piece of wood with a handle that my mom had painted silver and told me to write the word *paddle* on. Sadly, the one time she made me write a word fewer than a thousand times, I misspelled it. For years, we lived with a Padle on the wall.

The problem with the Padle was that my mother was reluctant to use it in a way that would actually be effective. She'd hold back and tap us with it softly. Wanting to make her feel better about the interaction, I would exaggerate my cries and yelps until she couldn't take it anymore.

Everyone I knew got spanked. My friend and comedian Chip Pope grew up in Texas, where they had a whole rack of belts hanging on the closet door, like something out of a *Saw* movie. His dad would let him choose the belt, like "Which torture instrument seems less hurtful to you?"

Like everything else, discipline follows trends. I don't think it's even legal to spank your kids anymore, at least not in any state that had a mask mandate during Covid. The new trend is validating your child when they do something wrong: "So you're saying you want to crack the television with a hammer—did I hear that right? I love you. You're so creative, you'll make a wonderful general contractor someday."

I'm sure the child psychologists have a reason to believe that positive reinforcement and validation are superior to threatening your kid with a Padle or telling them that if they don't behave you'll send them to live with their father. Since I've spent the last twenty years honing jokes about my pussy and not studying statistics on childhood development, I guess I just have to take their word for it.

But getting your kid to do anything—wear a mask, eat dinner, stop crying, pick up the dinner they just threw on the ground— has now turned into a series of micronegotiations that could end with her giving you a mini Bette Davis slap across your face. So, what do you do? How do you get them to bend to your will?

My research has revealed that there are three popular options for the discipline-curious parent: authoritarian ("because I said so"); authoritative ("here's why I said so"); and permissive ("whatever you say, my precious little genius").

I was raised by a "because I said so" parent; but now, living among the cheerful whites of Los Angeles, California, I see a lot of permissive parenting: super loving, very unstructured, totally ineffective.

I have a friend whose five-year-old was threatening the family dog with a meat tenderizer, but instead of screaming, "NO! DON'T HIT THE DOG!" my friend swooped in and cried out, "What an advanced culinary tool you've found! I love you, my little chef. And, oh yeah, we try not to bludgeon our pets, my perfect angel." Kind of burying the lede, if you ask me.

Another phenomenon of permissive parenting is what I like to call the Hey Buddy dad. We've all seen this dad at the playground or in the supermarket, trying to keep the vibe cool and calm while his child commits minor acts of violence and mayhem. "Hey, buddy, let's not poke your baby sister with those rusty nails, 'kay? Hey, buddy, she only has one set of eyes, let's not stick those nails in there, okay, buddy? Hey, buddy, I'm just gonna grab those nails from you, okay, buddy? Hey, buddy, can I get those nails? No? Okay, buddy, that nail went right through my skin into my throat. You're strong, aren't you, pal?"

As I write this, it definitely does seem more positive to give your kid a compliment when they are doing something wrong, but in the moment I've found it completely counterintuitive and impossible to implement. Besides, pretending that everything a kid does is wonderful is how we got a group of twenty-year-olds who live at home while they work on their personal brands.

My goal is to be an authoritative parent. Having rules, but explaining them. And then lots of communication as to why the kid is being disciplined. Still grounding them—but lovingly.

There's one minor flaw with this plan.

It's not always that easy to communicate with a child. It's more like—have you ever tried explaining the rules of cricket to a dog? And you only sort of know the rules of cricket? And the dog is busy trying to eat a plastic bag he found on the sidewalk?

After all, you don't become a Hey Buddy dad by only having to say "Hey, buddy" once to get your kid to stop stepping on your clavicle. You become a Hey Buddy dad because your kid cannot, will not, and does not listen.

It doesn't help that there are now all sorts of things we're not supposed to say to our kids. I recently read one of the many articles on the internet called something like "Ten Things to Never Say to Your Children." I realized I say every one multiple times a day, with the exception of "I'm going on a diet," but that's just because I'm both a gourmand and naturally thin.

These lists are another form of weird nostalgia. Instead of "27 Commercials Every Millennial Remembers" or "Remember These Beloved Actors from Your Childhood? They're All Really Old Now and Soon You Will Be Too," it's everything our parents ever told us, reimagined as a collection of what not to say to our own children.

No type of parent is safe from the harsh judgment of the list.

Protective parents? Never say "be careful," because this makes your kids stressed, which could actually lead to more accidents. Warning your child of imminent danger is apparently the equivalent of throwing a juggling pin at a blindfolded clown unicycling across a tightrope. I actually felt good about this advice because I never say "be careful." My go-to is: "Oh my god, no, you'll die if you do that!"

Trying to be supportive? "Let me help" is discouraged—you should let children do things themselves or they will always rely on you. Of course, when I was a child and did things myself, my mother helped me to a serving of Padle, so who knows how well this works.

It turns out that even the parents who do nothing but praise their kids are being positive in the wrong way. Did you know you're not supposed to say "Good job!" anymore? First of all, it sounds too much like "good dog," which is reserved for household pets who understand complicated British games. Worse yet, "good job" creates an environment where your child will do something only for your praise, which is apparently worth about as much as the pile of dog shit your cricket-loving terrier left in the backyard.

You're instead supposed to tell her you've noticed she's worked really hard on something, which frankly feels like a passive-aggressive way to tell your child you really aren't impressed with the end result of her finger-painting.

My personal favorite taboo parenting phrase is "stop crying." The experts opposed to this piteous request wonder if you'd tell your coworker to stop crying if they were upset. Well, no, but I also don't wipe my coworker's ass before tucking him into bed. (At least, not since the #MeToo movement.)

When it comes down to it, trying to reason with children and treating them as your peers is endowing them with qualities they don't have. Kids are barely human. They have the attention span of a dog, the legs of a cat, the balance of a penguin, and the desire to make mischief of one of those naughty monkeys at a Thai temple. They are like some kind of hybrid monster from Greek mythology.

If you have a kid, you're likely aware of the broken-record repetition required to get them to do anything. "No, you can't." "No. I said no. You cannot do that." "Absolutely not, no." "No!" "Okay, fine, you can play with the paring knife while we drive."

You're not having a rational, good-faith conversation with a stable individual. You're negotiating with Donald Trump. So, what do you do?

During the pandemic, I went to visit a preschool with my then-two-year-old and I told her she could have a piece of candy if she kept her mask on the whole time. (Imagine how many lives could have been saved if Dr. Fauci had tried that with Trump.)

The teacher overheard me and said, "I wouldn't bribe her."

"Well, I'm trying to get her to wear a mask," I responded while kneeling in the sand, dangling Swedish Fish over my daughter's head like she was a trained porpoise.

"You will learn other ways to get her to do things than giving her candy," the teacher said. It was our first outing in months, and my primary goal for my toddler was for her to not get a disease while we took a tour on which the main stops were a shoe-disinfecting station and a swing set the kids used to use when there wasn't a massive global pandemic raging and they were still allowed to touch things.

I thought this was a little rude of the teacher. I left that meeting feeling like I didn't know what I was doing. Giving my daughter candy to do things was so easy. *Am I a bad parent?* I wondered, feeling shamed.

The truth is, as the world's number one dad, former president and reality show host Donald Trump, surely knows: bribes work. You're definitely not supposed to say, "No dessert until you finish dinner!" But that's literally how I've gotten my child to eat any dinner ever. I don't really understand how *not* to use bribing.

Threats can work too, especially if delivered properly. (Another Trump tip.) No kid is like, "I should listen to Dad because he's a reasonable man and I should love and respect him." They're like, "I am scared because this man's voice is loud. I'm going to do what this large person says."

(The experts also say not to raise our voices too loudly, as it demonstrates lack of control. But you know what's scarier than a parent who yells at their kids? One who whispers.)

The big problem with threats is that they can easily backfire. If you take away your kid's iPad for the entire weekend, for example, you're only hurting yourself. You'll never be able to entertain them as well as a ninety-minute video of two nine-year-olds in the Philippines feeding Play-Doh to Barbies dressed like the characters from *Frozen*. Remember: screen time is not just a child's privilege; it's a parent's right.

That's sort of the big lesson of discipline. It's not just for your kids—it's for you.

Discipline is neither a dirty word nor tantamount to abuse. Discipline is just a way to positively influence your child's behavior, while simultaneously making them annoy you less. And then when they annoy you less, you will become less likely to engage in behavior toward them that *is* tantamount to abuse. Everyone wins.

The whole idea that you can get your kid to do things without threatening or punishing or bribing them presupposes that you have nothing to do but parent. I would love to reframe my dialogue with my child and never say "Good job!" or "Be careful!" but I don't have limitless supplies of patience, time, and energy. Sometimes you need shortcuts. The truth is, my kid wouldn't eat dinner or take naps or behave if I didn't bribe her and ply her with presents and then threaten to throw those presents in the trash if she doesn't go to sleep right now.

Not every aspect of parenting is magical. I didn't cherish the time my kid almost swallowed a penny. Or the time she peed on my banquette while I was trying to potty train her naked in the kitchen. (Shout-out to *Oh Crap!*)*

We can't expect our kids to adapt to the metaphysical truth of the universe without more than a little nudging. Should I just gently guide my child through good decisions and doing everything herself, regardless of the fact that it takes her four hours to put on her shoes if I don't offer to help? This asks too much of the average parent.

In a strange way, discipline is not about control—it's about letting go. Our kids may not always be who we want them to be, but for a while—at least until their hands are strong enough to unlock baby gates—they can do what we want them to do. Because no matter what we do as parents, we still can't control everything. You can follow every parenting tip the internet has to offer, but the world will still bring your child heartache.

I'm sure I've mentioned that I was a child actress in this book about as many times as someone reminds you they went to Harvard. I am forever grateful to my mother for standing in line and signing me up for theater classes when swimming was full. By twelve years old, I had been acting in plays in the evenings, weekends, and sometimes Wednesday matinees for two years. I knew I wanted to be an actress, but I was tired of the theater. I wanted to be a movie star!

---

* As in *Oh Crap! Potty Training* by Jamie Glowacki, savior of parents everywhere.

My cinematic debut was in a film called *Personal Foul*. It was shot in my hometown of Rockford, Illinois, and it starred David Morse and Alan Arkin. The movie took place in a school, so they were going to need a lot of kids. Having paid my dues treading the boards and taking tap dancing lessons on Saturdays, I thought the film would be the perfect way to pivot my regional theater stage career into Hollywood stardom.

I auditioned for the biggest part for children, and I got it. I would be in one scene: two kids in a hallway, exchanging items from their lunchboxes. It was the role I'd been preparing for since kindergarten.

I arrived on set with a fresh perm and in my cutest, brightest, most colorful Esprit outfit. The director showed us where to stand and I took it all in stride, like the old pro I'd become. At twelve, I was already a veteran of the theater, dropping terms like "blocking" and "mark" to my costars, while thinking to myself, *I bet David Morse hasn't done much theater.*

As soon as the director called, "Action!" I pranced to my mark and said my first line. (Which I nailed, naturally.) Then as I was walking to my next mark, my lunchbox came open and its contents tumbled to the ground. "CUT!" I yelled, even doing the correct hand motion. The director ran over and got within an inch of my face to tell me, "You are the actor! You never yell 'Cut!' "

I remember being embarrassed, mainly because he said it really loudly. But, as a pro, I took the director's note and got through the scene, knowing all my lines, hitting all my marks, and, most important, not yelling "CUT!" again. I wrapped my day, but not before getting a lot of compliments on my fluorescent fuchsia wardrobe.

Almost a year later, I had been anticipating the premiere of *Personal Foul*. I was ready to move to LA or New York and get started on my film career; I had done all I could in Rockford. I was the resident child actor—I had been on the cover of *Rockford* magazine, interviewed at a Wendy's about what it was like to juggle a life in the theater with the fourth grade. A feature in *Variety* was surely next.

I knew that seeing my face up on the big screen would validate my desire to become the next Marilyn Monroe. Fantasies of going to every screening at the mall and standing up and yelling, "That's me!" to the captive audience played over and over in my head. I had invited my entire extended family to the premiere: grandparents, cousins, and other loosely related Italians filled up two entire rows of the theater.

I watched excitedly for my face to appear on the screen. After an hour and a half of Natasha-less close-ups, the credits rolled. Big, hot tears started streaming down my cheeks at the same speed as the credits. I looked to either side of me at my confused family, who didn't understand why I wasn't in the movie.

I bring up this story for two reasons. One, to remind you that I was a child actor who worked with an Academy Award winner before I'd even hit puberty. And two, to show that you can do everything you can for your child, but you can't guarantee they won't be cut out of the movie. (It was a small comfort at least to be able to add *cutting room floor* to my industry lexicon.)

We don't want to be too hard on our kids, but we also can't be too hard on ourselves. That's why I try to remember to reward myself with small luxuries, like taking a hot bath, ordering from a favorite restaurant, or giving my daughter her iPad so I can look at my phone in peace for an hour. She may not always have earned that screen time, but I certainly have.

FEAR AND LOVE

"Fear is the parent of cruelty."
—JAMES ANTHONY FROUDE

'm not a fearful person. I've lived my life making one reckless decision after another. I love travel, drugs, parties, and picking fights with bros, ideally all in one night.

Life to me was about risk. That's what made it worth living. So how do I today find myself constantly worried about, for example, choking? Before I had a child, I don't think I thought about choking . . . ever? I mean, maybe during certain porn but that's it. I've eaten approximately sixty million meals and never worried about choking once. Now I slice grapes into fourths and stare at my daughter's windpipe as she chews.

We don't become mothers to stay the same—at least, that's what my therapist told me. And motherhood has changed me in countless ways. I now always have snacks (sliced, diced, or minced into easily swallowable sizes) in my purse. I'll never need an alarm clock again. I even know the name of Peppa Pig's father (Daddy Pig—lazy British writers).

These are big changes. But the biggest change is that I've kind of become a scared person. Childbirth may not have turned my pussy giant (thank you, planned C-section!), but motherhood has turned me into a giant pussy.

I started before I even had a kid. I spent three years of my life afraid that I wouldn't be able to get pregnant.

Anything that anyone on the internet ever said could get you pregnant, I tried. Eat baby bananas, drink whipping cream, eat sticks of butter: tried, tried, tried. I drank some tea that tasted like tree bark that a dog took a shit on. I took weird round pills that an acupuncturist sold me for $85 a bottle. I practiced yoga for fertility, tried reiki for fertility, ate for fertility. Sometimes I would even have sex with my husband for fertility.

I was trying to get pregnant the old-fashioned way (silent missionary with no eye contact), but I also had embryos in a freezer in Westwood. Moshe had "busted" all over my original eggs I had frozen, and we were left with a few Motasha embryos that we were told would be our last resort. (Harvesting reproductive material is my favorite last-minute invasive medical procedure.)

My fertility doctor had strongly discouraged me from using these frozen embryos, however. He said they each had less than a 30 percent chance of working, and although I was already forty-one, I should still try to squeeze everything I could out of my last naturally fertile days. The doctor said to think of those frozen eggs as a savings account and my own eggs as a checking account. In retrospect, I realized what he meant to say was, "Think of your furiously diminishing fertility as a way of helping *my* checking and savings accounts."

I got a book that explained you could only get pregnant the exact moment you're ovulating. It suggested I stick two fingers up my vagina to look for an egg-white consistency. Are you grossed out yet? That's exactly why the author of the book says more women don't know how to check when they're fertile: because of people like you, thinking, *Ewww*, right now.*

The book instructed me how to make a V with my fingers once they had a "nice layer of discharge," and if what came out of me had the consistency of egg whites, it was time to have sex. (Or make my famous vagina meringue pie.)

In addition to tracking my very irregular period and fingering myself every time I peed, my doctor recommended intrauterine insemination, or IUI. If you're unfamiliar with all of the ways science can help you get pregnant, IUIs are when you have some of your husband's sperm ready and on tap for the nurses to inject into you in case he's at the Laugh Stop Albuquerque during one of your "egg white" days.

I probably wasted two years and tens of thousands of dollars trying to get pregnant "naturally" after forty-one. Nothing takes

---

* The book is called *Taking Charge of Your Fertility* by Toni Weschler, MPH, if you want to give it a try.

the fun out of sex faster than taking your temperature, peeing on a stick, and trying to make sure your husband's semen doesn't fall out of you immediately after sex. I finally decided to defy my doctors and take the plunge into my fertility savings account to see if either of my embryos would make it.

And one did.

I'd spent the past three years being afraid I wouldn't have a kid and I finally got pregnant with my frozen embryo. I figured the worrying would stop. But it had only just begun.

Once I was pregnant, a friend suggested I join her at a birthing center in Orange County (or birthing *boutique*, as it says on its website), where I imagine midwives feed you figs and you walk around and think beautiful thoughts until the baby starts to gently fall out of you, at which point you're transitioned into a warm bathtub with orchids floating in it where you have your dream vaginal bathtub birth.

And as much as I hate to leave my bathtub for any reason, a vaginal bathtub birth was not in the cards for me. I was informed by my doctor that I had to give birth in a hospital because things could definitely go wrong—I was too "geriatric" to take any risks. As an almost-senile woman about to give birth, I had to take certain precautions, like being in a sterile medical facility with every blood type on tap and only getting cut open under fluorescent lights. If there were any complications, I was already at the hospital.

But any peace the easy access to on-demand plasma transfusions brought me was fleeting. My fear was off to the races. I was afraid of giving birth. I was afraid of contractions. I was afraid of miscarrying. I was afraid the baby wouldn't have all ten fingers and toes. I was afraid the weird thing on her belly button wouldn't come off, I was afraid that the soft spot in her head wouldn't close, I was afraid to breastfeed because it might ruin my tits, I was afraid to stop breastfeeding because it might ruin my child, I was afraid she would get a cold, I was afraid she would get coronavirus. And, of course, choking. I was afraid of choking.

I also have a feeling that the older my daughter gets, the more there'll be to terrify me. Just this week alone, I've worried about: sneaker waves (google it if you are into fear porn); ticks; leaving the gas on; mountain lions; screen time; and whether my daughter is getting bathed in lead from our pipes every time I wash her hair. A rotating cast of worries circles my brain on a daily basis. I was not emotionally prepared for this! I thought I'd read every book about fertility and pregnancy and childbirth and early childhood, and they all failed to mention that I'd also be giving birth to an eternal fear.

Being a parent is like being in a horror movie. You manage to survive Freddy, but Jason is waiting in the kitchen—and he wants to drop out of middle school to go live in a hype house in the Hollywood Hills with a group of fellow tweenfluencers he met online. How did I go from whitewater rafting with no helmet so I still looked cute to slapping a less-than-fully-cooked hot dog out of my child's hand and screaming, "DON'T EAT THAT!"

Is it because I'm a woman? Sure, I've met one or two "Don't eat that!" dads. But it's often the mom who takes it upon herself to be scared. My husband seems to love our daughter as much as I do with so much less of the fear. Is it because women are intellectually superior and more complex than men, which allows us to multitask and endows us with the ability to think many steps ahead? Or are women more fearful because we lack upper-body strength?

Maybe it's generational: our foremothers seemed to be a hardier bunch than we are. I suspect my grandma, for one, was too busy Spray 'n Washing *sugo* stains from the starched collars my grandpa wore to his frequent business dinners to be afraid of much.

Nana's father was a Sicilian farmhand in New Orleans (he eventually bought the farm—and I don't mean that euphemistically) and gave her his blessing to marry Papa, the upwardly mobile son of a baker from Torrino. Papa brought her back to Rockford, Illinois, where she proceeded to have seven children while he sold insurance by day and sometimes evening (or so it would appear from his many missed evening meals).

Nana was very efficient. She bottle-fed all seven kids and spaced out their births so they could take care of each other. Aunt Diane, the eldest, was in charge of the little kids (including my dad) all day, while her other two sisters cleaned the house. Their hard work left time for Nana to pursue her true passion: ironing.

To Italian men, properly pressed clothing is as important as a good sugo recipe (Nana also had one of those). A lot of my early memories have ironing boards in them. I remember my mother ironing my dad's dress shirts so he could go to a nightclub while she stayed home with the three kids. My dad owned different nightclubs throughout the years and always had to look his best. When I was twelve, I was put in charge of ironing the Catholic school uniforms my brothers and I wore. No wonder I was so desperate to return to the theater.

I come from three generations of women who ironed for men, so I used to wonder if men got married just to have a live-in dry-cleaning service. What an amazing feat for women's liberation to no longer be expected to iron a man's clothes all day so he can look good while he's out, probably cheating on you.

The point is, if I were running a Fluff & Fold from my house while making three meals a day for ten people, I probably wouldn't have time to let all of the little fears that torment me take root.

Maybe that's it: I just have too much time on my hands. Everyone knows there's nothing more dangerous than a white woman with too much time on her hands. After all, what is a Karen but a white woman with an empty calendar? Who are all these white ladies who are just going on walks all day, looking for imaginary crimes to report?

On the other hand, my mom was busy trying to figure out how to leave a bad relationship, feed three kids, and get a job without a college degree or any money for a babysitter, but she still found a little time to worry. When I was in my twenties, she'd always want me to call her whenever I landed after an international flight. I always thought she was treating me like a toddler. "I'm fine!" I'd say and roll my eyes. "It's just a trip to England. It's basically America with weirder candy bars."

But she couldn't help being just a little afraid for her daughter. What could possibly happen to me? *I'm an adult*, I'd think, *not a three-year-old opening up cabinets, sucking on Tide Pods.* I was old enough to know better.

Perhaps I'd worry less if I had more kids. Was my nana not afraid because she had so many kids? Or was she seven times more afraid? Judging from her joie de vivre, she wasn't. And that doesn't seem uncommon for parents of multiple children. My friends with two or three kids often say to me as I helicopter-parent, "I used to be like that too." Then they go let their kids run around barefoot in a lumberyard.

I'm a woman with one child, and I'm older, so this is probably it for me. Meanwhile, a man can start another family basically up until the last split-second he's alive. A ninety-five-year-old man can literally become a father and die of a massive heart attack at the exact same moment. (I assume that's how most men hope to die.)

One thing I do know for sure is that fear sells. I learned that early on my path to motherhood. Here's one conversation I had at the beginning of my conception journey:

"This is the last session, but if you renew for another ten today, your ninth session will be free!"

"How much is one session again?"

"One hundred ninety dollars."

And then I handed over my credit card to a forty-five-year-old hippie/acupuncturist/scam artist. I don't know where I'd heard that lying in a hyperbaric chamber could help make you more fertile—I live in Los Angeles and work in Hollywood, so it could have been literally anywhere I go on a daily basis—but I was desperate.

There's an entire category of news that's basically "horrible shit that can happen to your kids." Facebook is now half elderly women dabbling in racial extremism and half mothers commenting about a two-year-old who got flesh-eating bacteria from using a public restroom that looked clean.

There are plenty of businesses/acupuncturists willing to sell you a product/fertility massage that will address your fears, so it's profitable to stoke them as much as possible. If your toddler hasn't tried cuisines from each continent by the time she turns three, she'll never develop a sophisticated palate. If you wash your baby's cloth diapers (always cloth, goddammit, unless you want your kids to live in a world where the ocean has been replaced by a landfill) with liquid fabric softener, he'll one day only be able to experience pleasure by rubbing up against strangers on the subway.

We're told we can avoid these and many other even worse outcomes if we just buy the right food/toys/educational experiences. I'd pin a lot of my fears on the news and the internet, but this entire phenomenon—selling fear because fear sells—could describe all late-stage capitalism, or at least that's what I heard my husband say into his headset while he vaped through nine hours of *Apex Legends*.

Before having a kid, I thought I was fearless. I've always jumped into the fire my whole life. I loved doing impromptu things. Once I saw a friend at an audition and she was about to leave for Africa and told me another friend had just dropped out of the trip. "I'll go!" I screamed, and then immediately got $900 worth of vaccines shot up and down my arms and hopped on a plane almost the next day. Stand-up comedy on a yacht in Thailand? Performing at a bar in Paris in exchange for a bed at a youth hostel? Anytime anyone invited me anyplace where I could see the world, I said yes.

There is such freedom in living your life for yourself. Only really being *responsible* for yourself. I wonder if I traded this in for the love I have for my child. Is there a way to get back to my pre-motherhood personality? Pre-motherhood Natasha wouldn't think twice about bringing her baby to Bangkok for some stage time and free shrimp. Where did that lady go?

I think the real reason I'm so afraid for my child in a way I wasn't afraid for myself is that I love her even more than I love myself. (Don't tell my agent.) I didn't want to be murdered in the Australian outback (or survive a murder just to pay market-rate rent in Manhattan), but that was a risk I was willing to take.

That's sort of the big irony of the whole thing. I want to love my daughter so much that she feels secure enough to be fearless, to make the types of decisions and choices that will both make me proud and keep me from sleeping peacefully through the night for the rest of my life.

PARENTING IN
ENVIRONMENTAL PANIC

"Maybe we should protect our kids by not having them."
—TRAVIS RIEDER, BIOETHICS PROFESSOR AT JOHNS HOPKINS

"I believe the children are our future."
—THAT SONG FROM THE 1980S

$\mathcal{S}$ince March 2020, I've gotten more six-paragraph texts about HEPA filters and fears about death than I have in my life. The mental calculus and amount of scientific data we were all required to understand in order to make simple decisions concerning Covid was overwhelming. I failed science for a reason. (It's boring.)

I guess I secretly wanted someone I trust to tell me what is safe for my family, but Covid wasn't like that. *You* have to figure everything out because everything is politicized and everyone agrees misinformation is permeating society like an agent's bad cologne.

So now the person who got solid Ds in science (me) has to read a million articles about aerosol BPMs (or whatever they are called; I don't feel like googling it).

I mean, of course that is going to make one depressed. I'm filling my days downloading data so I can decide if going to a playground is too risky a proposition for my three-year-old who is sitting at home, looking out of a window, and murmuring, "Other people?" like an extra in *Oliver!*

Am I potentially setting her up for Long Covid if I get her bangs trimmed? If we sit inside a restaurant, could that lead to her permanently losing her sense of taste and smell? Will sending her to preschool in just a cloth mask land her in an ICU bed? How do I navigate this? And how do I remain calm? One time, during a surge, I put an N95 mask on my daughter's face and she asked, "Mom, when the coronavirus is over, can I wear any mask I want?"

Not only was I unable to get to my creative work during the pandemic, the weight of all these decisions wore on my mental health. My creative energy seemed to go into folding underwear. And not even my own underwear! I want my child to see me being creative and carefree, not Lysol-ing the oranges.

Come to think of it, everything you do to try to be healthier, if you look hard enough, has a bad side to it. I tried to switch from milk chocolate to dark chocolate, but did you know that 90 percent of cacao is harvested by child labor in Africa? I tried to stop eating meat, but then I found out a lot of plant-based vegetarian burgers have more calories, fat, and salt than a regular burger from Carl's Jr. I tried to drive away the bad energy from eating all of those delicious Monster Angus Thickburgers with a little palo santo, but then I learned its popularity is adding to deforestation and its possible extinction.

No matter what you do, you're doing it wrong.

And we always know when we're screwing up, thanks to the internet.

My phone is like that psycho you try to avoid at the party who is excited to give you bad news every time you talk to them. It's not that I don't *want* to hear about your widowed mother's new boyfriend's son selling your dead dad's prized collection of silver dollars on eBay, but at least let me get a drink first.

Every time I look at my phone, there is some alert that a child has drowned, been locked in a garage with only a dog collar on, or been decapitated by her father as she cries, "Daddy, no!" (An actual story.) It's almost like my phone knows I have a baby (in addition to every single other thing about me) and then purposely shows me the worst news stories to terrify me so I'll download more mind/body apps.

Which I then of course do—but did you know that meditation apps in particular share and sell more of your data to spam than any other app? I guess that's what you get for using your phone to meditate.

We have to deal with all of this, PLUS scientists across the board say the world is ending. There are apparently two potential outcomes for earth in the next thirty years: catastrophe or chaos.

And the United Nations says if humanity continues to produce, consume, and function as we're doing now, we're headed straight toward catastrophe. Sorry, chaos! You sounded like fun, you messy bitch.

Here's a cheerful thought! What if our children are the first generation to know that the world is ending in their lifetime? I certainly didn't know this shit when I was growing up.

Science was always my least favorite subject. You see, I went to a public middle school that decided all students should be categorized into a specific group.

There was BD (Behavior Disability), LD (Learning Disability), Eureka (the smart kids), CAPA (Creative and Performing Arts), and "Regulars" (everybody else, I guess).

My brother Louie was a BD/LD double major. I was too obnoxious to be considered smart but obviously wasn't going to let them call me regular, so my mom put me in CAPA. Plus, I was already a seasoned child actor. Our electives were art, modern dance, choir, theater, tech theater, and fiber art. I remember bringing home various useless wicker baskets I had weaved in fiber art class, as a gift to my mom for helping me escape being a "Regular."

We CAPA kids were always getting special treatment. I have distinct memories of being allowed to skip science class in order to choreograph an important modern dance piece. We were the future divas of the world; we didn't have time for SCIENCE!

I'm grateful for the CAPA program. It helped me believe in

myself as an artist while simultaneously keeping my knowledge of science hovering at a fourth-grade level.

My complete lack of interest in all things science continued through high school and college. I went to college for nine years because I paid for it myself and could only afford state schools. As I moved around trying to get closer to New York, a lot of my credits didn't transfer. I had to take science summer school at Brooklyn College because I couldn't get my BA in theater criticism without a certain number of science credits. (I still don't understand why I needed to take college chemistry to be able to recognize a bad performance of *Cat on a Hot Tin Roof*.)

I was very stressed until a counselor tipped me off that in summer school, a D was considered passing. And I was proud of my passing D: I didn't care about anything but becoming a great actress, getting an apartment in Van Nuys, and finally being able to audition for Doritos commercials.

I was in my late twenties before I had even heard of the possibility that the earth was melting. Today's kids aren't so lucky. There's now a scientific consensus that the lives of our children are going to be very difficult. There's even a group called "birth strikers," women who refuse to have children due to the severity of the ecological crisis. (Or at least, that's what they tell their disappointed Jewish mothers.)

According to the strikers, having even one less child is a more effective way of cutting down a person's carbon footprint than recycling, driving an electric car, being a vegetarian, or using renewable energy. A kid is like a human Hummer.

While I was busy not learning about science, a movement to stop the perpetuation of the human species was blossoming. Zero population growth, or ZPG, is a movement that believes that a constantly increasing population is actually responsible for many of our problems: pollution, violence, loss of values and individual privacy. Founded in 1968 by sociologist Kingsley Davis, ZPG gained momentum in the eighties. Perhaps it was even taught in private schools, but I had certainly never heard of it.

Today, like so many of us, I can recite all the dismal facts. Two-thirds of the world's wild species are disappearing, the Greenland ice sheet is melting faster than we thought, and sea-level projections are getting revised upward every year. The air is not good inside and the air is not good outside.

Here in Los Angeles, we now have only three seasons: awards, pilot, and wildfire, which has gone from four months out of the year to seven months out of the year. I'm currently writing this chapter from my husband's RV, which we drove ten hours north to escape the bad air quality caused by this season's unprecedented fires.

I wasn't always so psyched to have a giant trailer parked in my backyard. I told my husband that if he dies, he has to leave it to someone else because I don't need the hassle. But now I'm glad we can drive away in a portable house every time the air quality plummets from a wildfire started by a gender reveal party.

So here we are: like a rickety RV on a stretch of the Pacific Coast Highway that's down to one lane because coastal erosion has literally eaten the road, the world is speeding through chaos, fast on its way to catastrophe. And what a fun ride it's been! There's racial injustice, they are *still* trying to overturn *Roe v. Wade* (by the time this is published, it might have already happened), there are more homeless people than ever before, and plastic is filling up the landfills faster than I can read an article about how a toddler just got rat-bite fever.

So why have a fucking baby?

Welcome to the burning, melting world, my sweetest darling!

Don't get me wrong, I'm so glad I had my child. She makes my life so much better. And it's true: I can't imagine my life without her. She spreads joy just by existing. But was it fair for me to bring her into this world?

Well, I hope so, because that ship has sailed. And this isn't a book about *not* having children. So what do we do now that all these kids are here?

I personally want to raise someone cool so there aren't only idiots to inherit the earth. You can't let those people have all the kids!

If we're going to find the off-ramp between chaos and catastrophe, we need a generation (or two or three) of kids who won't make the same mistakes we've all made. Environmental degradation, excessive consumption, that roughly five-year period at the end of the last millennium when women in their twenties regularly wore baby tees and JNCO jeans and it was considered "hot." We can't let any of that happen again.

But how do you raise a child who knows better? How do you raise an ethical child?

When Ruth Bader Ginsburg died, we were quarantined with another family. My husband came in and delivered the news discreetly to the other adults. Without missing a beat, our friend Susan immediately rushed to her nine-year-old daughter and said, "Oh my god, honey, Ruth Bader Ginsburg just died! This is terrible! They're going to put in another Supreme Court justice and it's going to take away our rights as women and we will never be free!" The nine-year-old immediately started crying and screamed, "I HATE DONALD TRUMP!"

My husband and I exchanged wide-eyed glances. We all want conscious, aware, maybe even activist children—but isn't that a lot of pressure to put on them?

It felt weird to burden kids with our own political anxieties, indoctrinating them to believe as we do. What if your kid just wants to have fun? Political awareness is important, but we don't want our kids to be neurotic and joyless. Have you ever seen a seven-year-old in a pussy hat? It's a bad look. Okay, maybe this is a privileged outlook, but seriously the hats are ugly.

The world is scary and in desperate need of repair, but the future of our planet and everything that lives on it just feels like a heavy load to place on tiny shoulders.

Being an ethical person is also about a lot more than having the right politics. Do you feed your dog sustainable organic dog food, but then let it take a shit in the neighbor's yard? You can tell a lot about a person by what they do with their dog's shit.

"Good" people aren't always considerate people. Just because you have a *Free South Africa* flag on your front door doesn't mean you aren't a horrible upstairs neighbor, rudely wheeling your office chair around until four in the morning on some Adderall-induced work bender like you're Alex P. Keaton, all while I'm trying to sleep. (Sorry, PTSD flashback from my studio apartment days.)

Teaching your kids the right political beliefs isn't enough. You can be on the most ethical, righteous, correct side of a political issue and still be a total piece of shit as a person. One of the biggest donors in Democratic campaign history, Harvey Weinstein, is a serial rapist. And, I would venture to guess, doesn't pick up his dog shit.

Even among those of us who aren't liberal sex criminals, we don't always set the examples we'd want our kids to follow. Like, I want to compost but I don't *want* to compost. It's hard to tell my daughter, "Daddy and I only throw our carrot peels and other food waste in the regular trash because we don't want an open bin that smells like rotting feces in the middle of our kitchen. But when you grow up, you should definitely compost. It's the right thing to do."

Ultimately, there's a difference between social values and personal values. You don't want your kid to grow up to be one of those people who lecture everyone about the dangers of social entitlement but are themselves personally entitled.

And there are so many personal values I want to instill in my kid that are nonpolitical. Are you kind? Helpful? Polite? Thoughtful? Generous? Do you try to make people feel better? Do you want to help those in need? Do you—oh, baneful word!—SHARE? Try not to be human pollution—you know, the kinds of people who consume and consume. Teach your child that it's wrong to want all the money for yourself. Do we really need billionaires?

As a mother, I feel like my goal in life is to make sure my daughter doesn't experience any pain. I have one child. Of course I want to protect her from pain and sadness and discomfort. Why would I want her to experience any of that?

But is this good for her? The other day she started crying when I offered her milk. "Not cow milk!" she screamed. I immediately opened the fridge and offered all the other milks I could find: "Oat? Almond? Cashew?" As tears rained down her red face, my daughter kept crying, "NOT COW MILK!" I rattled off the absurd assortment again in a panicked attempt to stop her crying. All I wanted was for her "pain" to go away.

She finally started screaming, "OAT MILK!" to which I replied, "Vanilla or regular?"

And then I realized: WHAT THE FUCK IS WRONG WITH ME? Am I a nut-milk sommelier? And, worse, am I creating a monster? Am I going to raise a child who throws a fit at a restaurant because they don't carry full-cream donkey milk?

Maybe we're exposing these kids to too many milks. Maybe until you're eighteen you should only be aware of one kind of milk. College can be their opportunity to experiment with different milks. When I was growing up, we drank water for dinner.

My mom did not try to cater to every one of my whims and needs. If I had told my mom I wanted an alternative milk, she would've told me to get a job. And I have more integrity because of it. If you want to see a good example of what happens when you give a child anything they want, watch some TikToks of kids getting Bentleys on their sixteenth birthday.

The most challenging part of parenting for me is teaching my daughter limits and boundaries, when my instincts are telling me to cater to her whims and alleviate all of her pain—even if that pain is sort of ridiculous.

My husband and daughter and I were once on vacation, sitting in a hot tub. My daughter started crying loudly and sputtered out, "I want to sit there," and attempted to shift me from my place. I happily started to move—I didn't care where I was sitting.

But my husband said, "Absolutely not, that is your mother's seat, and if you want her to move, you have to ask politely." After another short bout of scream-crying, my daughter said, "Mom, can I please sit in your spot?" I moved, and she was happy. Crisis averted.

It was a good lesson, but it ran counter to my instincts, which were to just give my daughter exactly what she wanted. In the same way I don't like fighting with trolls on my Instagram page, I don't like fighting with trolls who are my daughter. But maybe if I always submit to her whims, she will turn into a brat. Shouldn't she be happy just to be in a hot tub? I didn't experience water that warm until I turned twenty-five.

It doesn't stop at spa seating arrangements. I want my child to feel empowered and autonomous, but does that mean I have to tell her everything she does is great—even if it means lying to her?

Before I had my own kid, I had been to many graduation ceremonies and "concerts" of my friends' kids. I was always amazed when these kids started singing completely off-key to standing ovations and gasps of wonder from the audience, made up primarily of their parents (and a few of their parents' friends who got bamboozled into attending a child's musical performance).

Where does it end? I realize a three-year-old might not have harnessed all of their singing powers yet, but telling an untalented nine-year-old they sing like Adele seems detrimental. Your child's random smashing of piano keys may kill at home, but they're going to be in for rude awakening when they audition for Juilliard with their rendition of "Chopsticks." ("It's not bad—it's *jazz*.")

I feel like I want my kid to know her talent level. If your child is a terrible athlete and they tell you that they want to go to baseball camp, is it better to say, "You're amazing, it's the ball's fault you can't hit it," or "Baseball camp is expensive and you're bad at baseball, it's a huge waste of money and it will just make you feel bad"?

I'm not offering an answer, but I feel like if you tried the latter, sooner or later your terrible baseball player might find what they're really good at.

When I was growing up, I certainly didn't get everything I wanted. I was raised to buy things myself, so I saved up money. I had paper routes, mowed lawns, did laundry, worked at a grocery store, made dinner, and ironed Catholic school uniforms as a daily routine. My husband says whenever I talk about my childhood, I sound like Cinderella.

But I'm glad I had the upbringing I did. I know parents who can't get a fourteen-year-old to put their dishes in the dishwasher. Maybe that's not unethical, but it's certainly not ideal. Since I cleaned so much as a child, I always thought one of the perks of having a kid was that they could help me clean up after my husband.

The point is, there's more than one way to end up a good person.

We want our kids to understand their responsibility to the planet and all the other people on it, but we also don't want them to believe that that planet revolves around them. (Our planet revolves around the sun. Thank you, fourth-grade science!)

There's an even more important, but subtle, distinction to be drawn. There's a difference between "you can have whatever you want" and "you can make the world whatever you want it to be." The former is a recipe for spoiled, entitled brats; but the latter is what we want our kids to believe, deeply and sincerely and unburdened by fear or doubt.

So I think again about my friend's daughter, crying her eyes out over the fact that Amy Coney Barrett will likely *still* be sitting on the Supreme Court when this nine-year-old has a nine-year-old child of her own. And I realize my friend was right.

What if parenting at the end of the world, in an ideal world, would be teaching our kids to fight the enemy? Who is going to fight for women's rights if not this nine-year-old future woman? (I find *future woman* a much more respectful term than *girl*.)

If I'd been told at nine that a bunch of smirking jerks were plotting to take away any of my rights, I'd have been furious. How early do you start teaching children, girls in particular, that they may grow up to be unable to control what they do with their own bodies? That people are going to treat them unfairly because of their sex or race? That they might not have clean drinking water or breathable air? That the planet is doomed—unless they do something about it?

My best friend from high school had kids about a decade before me, and I remember driving in the car with her and her kids and every time we would pass a *Dexter* billboard, she would do anything she could to distract her children from the bloodstained actor. She preferred that her kids didn't hear any stories about death. (There goes the entire Disney cartoon canon.)

I understand shielding young kids from images of blood and death, but sooner or later—and probably sooner—this new generation is going to know catastrophe or chaos. Why shield them from fairy tales if the actual world is grimmer than Grimm?

Maybe our responsibility is, if you are going to have a kid, to instill in it (yes, IT) the basics of antibigoted, earth-loving, joy-spreading behavior. Raise cute little *it* to fight for the earth, not destroy it. Encourage a generation of climate activists who will fight for conservation while simultaneously learning how to reduce their waste. A generation of humans who listen to science and don't care about all of the flies that composting invites into our lives.

Am I suggesting using women's bodies to create liberal warriors to fight for conservation, racial equality, and the right for all women to do what they want with their own bodies, and in some countries even be able to drive? Am I naïve to think I can create an ideal version of my young self in my daughter? Despite my best efforts, will she still grow up to worship Ivanka Trump or worse, run a #vanlife Instagram?

None of us know for certain the answers to any of these questions, so in the meantime, don't feel guilty for having kids and don't feel guilty if you don't. Have as many as you want and can afford and will help you with the dishes. With luck they'll all grow up to be model citizens, stewards of the planet who fight for racial justice and throw away their iPhones. And if we're lucky, they just might save us from catastrophe.

SEX, GENDER, AND CONSENT—BABY EDITION

"For real change, we need feminine energy in the management of the world. We need a critical number of women in positions of power and we need to nurture the feminine energy in men."

—ISABEL ALLENDE

*M*aybe she won't be a girl forever, but for now, my daughter is really into her vagina. She is obsessed with the idea that she and I are both girls, that we both have a vagina, and that we pee sitting down because we don't have penises.

She is often double-checking with me. "Wolfie is a boy, right, Mom?" "That's right." "He has a penis?" "Yes, dear." "And I'm a girl, so I have a vagina." "Uh-huh." "Why?" she asks. "Oh! Look! Is that a hummingbird?!" I say, desperate to change the subject to anything that has less obvious genitalia.

The truth is, I don't know *why* she has a vagina. Am I supposed to tell her it's because she's a girl? What if she feels like a boy inside? Or at the very least a boy-girl, which is how she often referred to herself when she was between two and three.

When my daughter's preschool told us they'd be introducing the concept of gender fluidity to the three-year-olds, I gulped a bit. What did that mean exactly? I love the idea of the girls becoming more like boys and the boys becoming more like girls, but I only understood the difference between sex and gender last week—how am I supposed to teach it to my kid?

I was pretty certain that I wanted to improve upon what I was taught about gender and sex as a child, and protect my daughter from the gender indoctrination most of my generation received from almost the moment we were born, the idea that either "you are a boy, you must be manly" or "you are a girl, act like a lady."

That indoctrination starts with how we dress—or, really, are dressed—as children. It seems impossible that there are still people who associate blue with boys and pink with girls, especially now that men's fashion has embraced pastels. When my daughter was six months old, my husband instinctively ripped off the huge pink bow a family member had put on her bald head. Not only did she not have any hair, that part of her head hadn't even grown together yet. That bow would have sunk right into her skull.

In the past, women were taught from a young age to wear bows in their hair, cross their legs, and wear clothes that restrained their movement. That's why in every black-and-white photograph of a female toddler, whether an Italian peasant or a blue-blooded

Vanderbilt, that little girl is wearing a dress. My daughter loves to climb trees, and I realized she can't wear dresses to school if she wants to hang upside down on the monkey bars.

Boys got to wear jeans and overalls, apparel that allowed them to run around and encouraged them to manspread. I never thought of my dad as all that masculine until I saw him sit on public transportation. He never takes up fewer than three seats. It doesn't matter what he's wearing—dress pants, board shorts, sarong—my dad sits with his legs open and his hands clasped between his thighs, simultaneously protecting his private parts and his pinkie ring and gold watch (i.e., jewelry for men).

I wonder: Would my dad *not* manspread if he had experienced more gender fluidity in his youth? What if his mom had put a tutu on him once in a while? If he was forced to brush a doll's hair, maybe he wouldn't have backhanded my mom when she ironed his shirts wrong.

Growing up as a girl in the Midwest in the 1980s, I experienced a lot of gender indoctrination. Besides swimming, I was never made to do sports (Or is it "play sports"? As a girl, they never even bothered to tell me how to say it) like my brothers; I was in charge of the cooking and cleaning and ironing, just like my grandma.

I identified strongly as a girl, even though I was often identified by strangers as a boy, thanks to my mother making me get a pixie haircut. "Pixie" sounds cute but is just a nice way of describing a haircut one razor-size above the one Britney Spears used when she shaved her head. People would often compliment my mom on the good behavior of her three sons. I remember my face flushing when a woman would refer to me as a nice boy when I would open the door for her at the mall. (Hello, lady, ever hear of culottes?)

I hated that haircut, but now that I spend much of every morning trying to bribe my daughter to let me brush her hair so she doesn't roll into preschool like she just came from an EDM festival in the Nevada desert, I understand why my mother took me to Cost Cutters to get the shortest style available for girls.

I might have looked like a boy, but I certainly didn't act the way boys were expected to act. I didn't know how to throw a ball, and I was always the last one picked for every sport we did. (Every sport we played? Why is this so confusing?) I loved anything gold, I wanted to paint my fingernails bright red, and I was always wearing my mom's heels around the house. I would shove balled-up socks in my shirt to give the illusion of double-F breasts. On the outside, I might have looked like a prepubescent boy, but inside, I felt like Mae West.

I desperately wanted to be thought of as a girl, so my mom did what any responsible mother in the eighties did when her daughter was being misgendered: she pierced my ears. I would always opt for the biggest fake ruby or emerald earrings, and after that I was never mistaken for a boy again. (Though I did occasionally pass as an Armenian toddler.)

My mom continued to be in charge of my hairstyle until high

school. Once I got to ninth grade, she finally let me retire the pixie and grow out my thin, flat, bodiless hair long enough to get a white-rod perm. Now I wasn't mistaken for a boy; I was mistaken for Aileen Quinn in *Annie*.

My hairstyle served as pretty reliable birth control up until around age fifteen, at which point I got a boyfriend, despite my grown-out perm. I was obsessed with one day having sex, but I kind of instinctively knew not to ask my mother about it. All she had ever told me about sex was not to do it. She did not seem to be a fan of my "developing" and especially did not like it when I wore tight clothes, particularly on my butt.

In fact, I had a pair of pants that my mom disapproved of so much, she actually drove them to a dumpster on the outskirts of town. I was known for doing quick changes into tighter, shorter, sexier clothes behind the air-conditioning unit outside in our yard, so an out-of-town dumpster would guarantee I would never try to squeeze my bubble butt into those forbidden pants again.

I knew I had sex too young because I still thought a blow job meant blowing on the penis, like it was a steaming hot bowl of soup. I remember being in the backseat of my boyfriend's car, thinking, *Okay, I guess I'll just blow on it?* So I huffed . . . and I puffed . . . and I greatly disappointed him. Fortunately some kind of ancestral sex instinct came rushing back to me and I started doing it right. Maybe I worked at a brothel in my past life? Oh wait, I worked at one in *this* life. It was in Australia, and I only answered phones, though, Mom, if you're reading this.

The day I turned sixteen, I drove two of my friends past the KFC where we usually had lunch and straight to the health department to get on the pill—what I like to call the Rockford Reverse Commute. I wanted to have sex but I would not be getting pregnant. I was a lot luckier than my mother. When she wanted to have sex, it landed her with three kids, forever tying her to what *Forbes* rated as one of the worst cities in America.

My husband had a very different upbringing. He was raised by his mom and grandma in the Bay Area. His mom gave him lesbian erotica when it was time to learn about sex, while his grandma would stop him in the hallway when he was sixteen and bringing home girls, to make sure he wasn't forgetting to make them "climax," too. (Thanks, Grandma Hope!) My husband grew up going to nude hot tubs with his mom and seems to not even notice when people are naked.

We were recently at a hot springs where everyone was naked, and three women with the most beautiful huge, natural tits casually struck up a conversation with us. By some strange, wonderful coincidence, my husband had a *lot* in common with these gorgeous ladies and we just had to talk to them and their six perfect breasts for an entire hour, which I used to subtly check their boobs for hairs or asymmetry, anything to make me feel better about my semi-perfect mom tits.

As we left, we were chased down by another woman. The top

of her one-piece had been pulled down, revealing two more pendulous, perfectly shaped hippie tits. We had basically walked into the lesbian erotica my husband grew up reading.

"Hey! I heard you know about surf spots around here?" she asked, and then she and my husband proceeded to talk for thirty minutes about where to surf, where to eat when you surf, where to surf after you've eaten, and so on. Every time she laughed at something my husband said, her perfect tits jiggled a little. She repeated everything he told her, like a waiter without a notepad who you know isn't going to remember your order. When she said she was going alone, I almost felt bad for my husband. He needs a surf buddy!

Poor guy. I'm sure his younger self would have loved to surf and eat shrimp tacos with this woman and her breasts all up and down the California coast. When we left, I told him that if it were me, I would've pulled up my one-piece when I approached a man and his wife. He said I sound like the dad from *Footloose*.

I imagine my daughter will be more like my husband, considering body positivity is on her preschool curriculum. And I do try to be open—I went to Burning Man four times! Okay, three times, but I count the time I went pregnant twice. All in all, we're doing our best to make sure our kid knows it's okay for girls to wear blue overalls, cool for boys to wear pink dresses, and weird to pierce a baby's ears. But the Rockford in me is hoping to slide in a little lesson about how girls don't pull their tits out at hot springs.

And that's where the lessons get a little more complicated. Because I want my daughter to know that gender fluidity is real—but so is sexism. And that misogyny is proving to be a hard habit for humanity to break.

Like many of your favorite A-list actresses, sexism is way older than you think. (Sorry. Sexist joke.) There is archeological and anthropological evidence that thousands of years ago the religions of the day were fertility cults centered around women. After men began to hunt and gather and we all started living in an agricultural society, men overthrew the matriarchy with their brute physical power. Basically, once they planted crops rather than gathered grubs, they needed to say, "This land where the wheat grows is *mine!*" And once private property was an established concept, it was just a tiny leap for a man's wife to be included in the property. "This woman where the baby grows is *mine!*" Alas, we have been in a patriarchy ever since, due almost entirely to men's superior upper-body strength and ability to thresh corn. It's as if the fate of humankind was decided by a push-up contest.

Since then, sexism has been ingrained in every part of society—particularly religion. I grew up Catholic, and women still can't become Catholic priests. (Maybe because they're less likely to molest the altar boys?) Converting to Judaism felt like an upgrade, in part because in some Jewish communities, women can become rabbis.

But not all Jewish communities. I once went to a synagogue in Israel where there was a giant divider down the length of the sanctuary, with two-thirds of the space set aside for the exclusive use of men. I took my seat in the third of the room where the women were quietly following along in their prayer books, while on the other side of the "wall," in the biggest part of the room . . . the men danced. And sang. It was literally a party, led by the rabbi. For all I know, they had a fog machine and strobe lights and a rotating dance floor over there—but I don't know because we weren't even allowed to look. The women didn't seem to care—maybe they'd become used to being on the other side of the velvet rope—but I found it hard not to feel "less than."

It's not just Jews and Catholics. Even the laid-back, super-chill Eastern religions your acupuncturist is always telling you she's been "really getting into," like certain forms of Buddhism, completely disregard and deemphasize the role of the mother. In all these years since the toppling of the fertility goddesses, why do the orthodox orders of the world's religions still insist on such a male-centered theology?

It's the same reason we have to ask: Why have young girls always been expected to wear dresses? Why was foot-binding ever a thing? Why do women in Afghanistan have to leave the house in a full-body burka? Why are there still countries where a woman isn't allowed to go to college? The answer is simple and the same for all of these questions: so men can control them. What will it take for men to stop thinking they have a right to women's bodies?

And it's not just religion. The world is full of male-centric ideas. My favorite might be polyamory. Right now, somewhere in the world, there's a man trying to convince a woman that having multiple sexual partners is man's natural state. Which is fine, until you throw a mother into the mix.

Opening up a relationship is not quite as thrilling for a lactating mom. Think of the logistics alone. You're supposed to find the time between laundry, grocery shopping, and keeping a tiny human alive with a substance oozing out of your body to belly up to the bar so you can meet a new person for your husband to fuck?

Every man's best argument for polyamory is that apes do it. That's right. Apes. That part of the pitch goes something like this: "Hey, honey? After studying apes [i.e., listening to five minutes of a "behavioral sexuality" podcast], I think you should let me fuck other women while you focus on the baby. Maybe you can join in too, when you're done pumping. It will be fun! You know, because of apes."

Is this where we are as a species? Taking our cues from animals that casually eat their own shit? Now, don't get me wrong, I know some women love polyamory and simian love triangles, but most of the people I meet who extol the virtue of non-monogamy are men I wouldn't spend a night with alone, much less at an ape orgy.

When I was born, activists were trying to add the Equal Rights Amendment to the Constitution. They were not successful, due at least in part to conservative women who argued that the ERA would mean women could get drafted into the military. Look, I get it: the army seems worse than camping. There are actually a lot of ERA debates from the 1970s on YouTube, where you can watch charming chauvinist William F. Buckley grill the feminists on how much artillery a woman will be expected to carry down to the barracks. We've come a long way since then. Men who don't believe women should have equal rights aren't allowed to talk about it on TV. They have to save it for their podcasts.

Feminism has been through a lot in my lifetime. I vaguely remember going through college in the nineties thinking I wasn't a feminist. In my memory, back then the feminists were always man-hating hordes picketing the quad in welder's uniforms. Am I proud of this early memory I probably share with Donald Trump and the late Shah of Iran? Not particularly, but it did make me think I wasn't a feminist—at least whatever misinformed version of what I thought the nineties version of a feminist was. To me, at the time, it all felt very anti-glamour and anti-feminine. I thought that to be a feminist, I had to act more like a man. Was there room for me in that movement? I mean, I couldn't help what I was attracted to. One of my first memories was painting my nails red, putting on a fake gold watch, and admiring the way the red and gold glistened on my hand. I remember thinking, *More of this, please.*

While my vision of what feminism was and wasn't contained a lot of flawed thinking, we're also now better able to recognize that the feminist movement hasn't always been as inclusive as it should be, leaving out the voices of women of color and working women and working mothers from less-advantaged economic backgrounds. For so long, so many of the spokespeople of the feminist movement were (and continue to be, in many cases) elite, educated white women. And they're not the only ones who could tear William F. Buckley a new one.

America still hasn't passed the Equal Rights Amendment, but we did get the #MeToo movement. A legally binding amendment to the United States Constitution might feel a little more official than, you know, a hashtag, but I feel hopeful that #MeToo will make the world a better place for my daughter. Basically, the more self-conscious men feel about pulling their dicks out at a party, the better.

I'm not sure men realize the extent to which women are under the constant threat of strange men whipping out and/or aiming their penises at them. It can happen anywhere: the sidewalk, the subway, a male comedian's dressing room.

My fear of men is baked into my psyche. We live by a wooded area, and sometimes I go for walks alone on the path that runs through it. If a woman passes, I smile, make eye contact, and nod my head. But if I see a man approaching, I immediately reach into my pocket and put my finger on my mace, or if he seems particularly nonthreatening, I'll grab my cell phone as a prop and start talking loudly, because if I nod and make eye contact, even the least threatening man might misread my gesture and think I want to give him one of my signature air-based blow jobs.

If men hadn't taken so much advantage of the fact that they have more upper-body strength and can easily pin down a woman, maybe I wouldn't tense up every time I saw one on a wooded path. Maybe if Little Red Riding Hood had been wearing jeans and a sweatshirt instead of an impractical cape that restricted her arm movement, she would've been able to get away from the Big Bad Wolf.

The truth is, I always want more women around me than men—even when they're topless strangers asking my husband for food truck recommendations in Ojai. I can only imagine how much more uncomfortable I would have been if those sexy ladies had been men. I'll take a half dozen perfect tits over three strange dicks any day.

In fact, I don't want to be near *any* strange dicks. Uber driver, cab driver, person sitting next to me on a plane: keep your strange dicks away from me. Once, on a plane, I sat next to a man who chewed sunflower seeds and spit them into an empty water bottle the entire flight. He didn't pull his dick out, but he did spray his seed all over the plane.

Police officer, political leader, children's gymnastics instructor, yoga teacher adjusting my body—woman, please! Gynecologist? I'll definitely take a woman.

When I was trying to have a baby, I had a male gynecologist who was angry that I had made a fertility appointment with one of his colleagues. In the middle of an examination, he told me, "You're going to have to pick a doctor, you know." Maybe we could talk about this after your fingers are out of my pussy, doc? It's hard to imagine a woman saying something so inappropriate and aggressive while I'm just trying to figure out how to have a baby. She knows the vulnerable state of being finger-blasted by a professional is not the time for a business negotiation.

What drives women is more interesting to me. Also, I've never seen a woman hold one of her nostrils and snort the contents of the other nostril into a plant—much less jerk off into one. (Thanks for that image, Harvey Weinstein.)

I'm glad that men are finally beginning to feel like they can't take advantage of women in the same way they used to, that they might get in trouble at work for how they speak to a woman, that they might get fired if they touch their coworker's butt or ask them to have sex, or that they might not get to do their extremely high-paying jobs for a couple of years if they decide they want to block a door and jerk off.

The truth is, #MeToo can only make this world safer, especially for the women who are little girls (or boys!) right now. Sure, it sucks for men that they can no longer act with misogynistic abandon in the workplace. But it's cool for women! Whatever it takes to put more women in positions of power, I'm all for it—even if it means there are fewer daytime safe spaces for men to ejaculate freely.

One thing is obvious to me: as a society, we need more women who believe they can become writers, directors, producers, doctors, lawyers, and artists.

I used to make fun of Oprah for being a megalomaniac, but it has since dawned on me how important it is for people of color to see other people of color reaching the heights, even if we define the "heights" as putting yourself on the cover of the magazine you named after yourself every single month. Representation isn't just important as a concept, it's inspiring. And I feel stupid for not knowing that. But it's okay to grow.

I was once helping with the edit of *Another Period* and I was having a hard time standing up to one of the male editors. He kept acting like he was in charge of the show. On the one hand, I had co-created the show, written it, helped produce it, and also starred in it. On the other hand, he was a man. So I guess it was kind of a wash.

I had been listening to Amy Poehler's audiobook, *Yes Please*, one morning before editing and she had described standing up for herself to a director at some awards show and it got me amped. I walked in, sat down in the editing chair, and waited for the editor to utter his first condescending remark.

It took about ninety seconds.

I stood up, walked over to him, and calmly explained that this was my project, not his, and if he wanted to talk to me like that he could look for another job.

I was in my late thirties and had never talked to a man like that. Ever! That's a long time to go without standing up for yourself. In retrospect, it was a little irresponsible for me to threaten to fire him, as we were on a very tight budget and replacing him would have been financially disastrous. But I thought I'd bluff—like a guy does! He apologized, his voice a little bit shakier now.

I don't know if I would have had the courage to talk to the editor like that if I hadn't heard Amy discussing standing up for herself. Women in power beget women in power. Women who stick up for themselves inspire women to stick up for themselves. Women who name magazines after themselves inspire women to have magazines named after themselves, which you know if you're reading an excerpt of this book in *Natasha Monthly*.

These are lessons I want to teach my daughter, and I hope they are also the lessons we're teaching our sons. Because maybe the lessons of gender fluidity can help make the world a little less sexist. Maybe the answer lies in making the men more like women and the women more like men. Isn't this what the Bronies* have been championing?

It's not impossible. As far as I can tell, they do a better job of teaching gender fluidity in Europe. I remember going to Amsterdam and all the men seemed like sophisticated lumberjacks. These strapping men read books, knew their way around a wine list, and could all perform impromptu plumbing with the toolbox they keep neatly inside a compartment on their bike. And I bet they don't even manspread.

---

* Adult male fans of *My Little Pony*.

CHRISTMAS IN MY HEART

"It's only once a year, sir."

—CHARLES DICKENS

*T*he amount of money of I've spent taking improv classes in LA is matched only by the number of mantras I've acquired over the years. To name a few: Om, Ram, Nam-myoho-renge-kyo, Hare Krishna, a silent transcendental meditation mantra I'm not allowed to tell you (although I can tell you that Ginger Spice was in my TM class).

I've chanted positive-thinking mantras all over Hollywood (shout-out to Florence Scovel Shinn!), I've been to Agape, I've watched and read *The Secret* (unironically), I hugged a hugging saint in a convention center, I got another mantra from some guy with a mohawk that everyone raved about until he got #MeToo-ed, and I've even been mildly hit on by Bikram himself (too sweaty). I believed more in the I Ching than I ever did in Catholicism. I tried everything. If my career had gone 28 percent worse, I would have tried Scientology.

I loved Ram Dass, whose main teaching seemed to be "work on yourself." The Buddhist chant I most connected with had as its end goal *Kosen-rufu*, which is essentially world peace through individual happiness. And how do you get individual happiness? By working on yourself! I wanted to reach my full potential as a human—and for a while, that didn't feel like it was happening.

When I moved to Los Angeles, I was thirty and I'd been a waitress for going on fifteen years. I had many aspirations for myself but felt stuck. That's around when I first tried to *Secret* my way into an acting job, not because I'm crazy, but because I thought being a working actor and a professional comedian would make me happy. (It did!) I sought out self-help books and memorized mantras because they seemed bigger than me. I didn't have professional mentors or financial help, so I had to find my own path to get through the pain of bringing strangers vodka tonics.

It's only years later that I've realized what I was really searching for were traditions. Mantras and meditations and personal practices are just daily traditions, right? And I wanted the sense of peace and security they would bring me.

When I was growing up, my mom definitely wanted more tradition in our lives. She would have loved for us to eat dinner together every night, but she was often working, so I'd end up microwaving for my brothers. Tradition is a luxury of time, and single moms with a bunch of kids do not have a lot of leisure time.

In the eighties, young women weren't on the internet; they were trying to work up the courage to divorce the men they accidentally married and had kids with. I'm proud that my mom was part of the first generation of women to say "fuck you" to their husbands in large numbers. Most kids I knew, most people in my family, and almost every comedian I know: their parents got divorced in the eighties. I just assumed that every child alive during the years 1979 to 1987 had a second family.

Before I got pregnant, I'd noticed that there were so many books on parenting, with such specific topics. Potty-training techniques from around the world, in case you ever find yourself in Oceania without your child's preferred PAW Patrol potty seat; cookbooks for ethical vegan toddlers with tree-nut allergies (a lot of hemp pancakes and glasses of lukewarm water); endless books on how to talk to your kids (Or not! Silent parenting sounds very relaxing).

But I never saw any books about how to actually *be* a family. Traditions are one of the biggest parts of becoming a family, and I had no guidelines for how to create them—until I became Jewish.

I'd always heard that Jewish men famously make the best husbands, so I'd wanted to marry Ad-Rock aka Adam Horovitz from seventh grade to sophomore year in college, and then Mike D aka Michael Diamond from sophomore year to senior year of college. (Sorry, MCA aka Adam Yauch! It wasn't personal, RIP.)

My own husband, Moshe (his real name, though also the name I'd make up for the archetypal Jewish husband), never asked me to convert to Judaism, but I knew he would be overjoyed if I decided to do it. It was an easy decision for me, as being Catholic was getting more and more embarrassing.

I liked that women could be rabbis and loved that Judaism welcomed questions. I still have PTSD from getting sent into the hallway every time I asked a question in Catholic school. (Mr. Heim, I really did want to know if Adam and Eve *actually* had sex.)

Throughout all my years in Catholic school, questions were discouraged. (Especially ones like "Why do the boys go on so many camping trips with Father Mike?") I was taught to obey what the nuns and priests said, accept it as law, and start practicing it myself. Meanwhile, Jews question everything! They've been arguing about whether or not you can eat lentils on Passover for more than two thousand years.

When the opportunity arose to not have to sheepishly say "Catholic?" every time someone asked me my religion, I jumped at the chance.

Conversion consisted of nineteen four-hour classes where the teacher, Rabbi Neal Weinberg (he insisted we address him by the full version of his name), had figured out a way to get people converted faster than anyone in Hollywood. He taught a class every night of the week, so that if you really wanted to become Jewish you could get it done in three weeks, like a juice fast. I took the three-month route.

Rabbi Neal Weinberg was a very knowledgeable, efficient, passionate Jew who loved converting people to Judaism. He made me want to be Jewish. It didn't even bother me that the class was full of hot Latina women marrying seventy-year-old millionaires. The degree of hotness was in direct proportion to how nice the husband's car was.

When my husband and I got married, I wanted to have the traditional Jewish ceremony from agrarian times that I had learned about in Rabbi Neal Weinberg's class. I wanted my wedding to include the *bedeken*, which is basically a gender-separated musical march that culminates in an unveiling of the bride, to make sure the groom isn't getting tricked into marrying the farmer's uglier daughter. I wore a napkin on my head; Moshe lifted it, said some Hebrew version of "Yep, that's her," and we walked to the wedding canopy.

We did it all, including the tradition of having sex right after we broke the glass. The purpose of this ancient rite is to confirm the virginity of the bride; after the couple has sex, the newlyweds emerge from their nuptial bed and celebrate the bride's annihilated hymen by presenting the bloody sheet to the townspeople.

I'm sure you can imagine my thrill when Rabbi Neal Weinberg explained this tradition; I was overjoyed that I could include such elaborate prop work in my wedding. After the ceremony (and the sex), my husband and I presented a pre-bloodied sheet that said "She's a Virgin" to our guests. Even the old people seemed to like it. Talk about a closer!

When I'd converted, the rabbi said the most important things for a Jewish life are: to keep Shabbat; to have a Jewish family; and *tikkun olam,* "an aspiration to repair and mend the world." I loved this idea, and it mirrored many of my own beliefs that I'd tried to follow through two decades of reading every self-help book ever written. All those years I'd been into *tikkun olam* and didn't even know it!

By far my favorite part of Judaism is Shabbat. For my gentile readers, allow me to explain. There's a dinner party every Friday at sundown called Shabbat where your husband brings you flowers and you bake bread, light candles, drink wine, get blessed, and have sex. Shabbat has it all: carbs, candles, cabernet, and cock.

As if that weren't enough, the next day the holiday continues and you have wine at lunch and take a long walk with your family, and when the sun goes down there's *another* party, Havdalah, where you celebrate that Shabbat is over. You drink more wine, pass around a nosegay, and sing a song for a good week to come. If it weren't for the temple parts in between, it would seem like a seventeenth-century fete. Or at least a dream Tinder date.

I love when my husband and I celebrate Shabbat. It made us closer when we were first married and has made us closer as a family now that we have a kid. Sometimes we cook dinner and say all the prayers, sometimes we forget that it's Friday and skip the whole thing, and sometimes we do a speed version of bread/wine/candles with our mountain of takeout containers and stare at our phones for the rest of the night. But we do something. The honorable Rabbi Neal Weinberg would be proud.

Lighting candles as a family once a week makes me so happy, because it's something I'm creating with my family, for my family.

We sometimes have more power over the lives we make for ourselves and our children than we think.

It's a little scary when you realize that everything you're doing could be establishing traditions for your child. After all, traditions are what we do, not what we'd *like* to do. You don't want your kid to remember that every Sunday, Mom and Dad would look at their phones and ignore their children for six hours. And she will always remember how you used to get an extra-large Coke at McDonald's every Tuesday and Thursday when she's forty and has lost both of her legs to diabetes.

Traditions are a way of telling your family, "This is how we choose to spend our special time." These traditions can feel like the things that make life worth living. Why else would people risk their lives during a global pandemic to throw a party for their nephew who just got a certification from nursing school? So much of daily life is drudgery. Tradition is an escape from that.

All that said, it takes a lot of strength to create your own traditions and stick with them. Becoming Jewish for me was about providing a framework for adopting and maintaining traditions that would elevate my family's quality of life. Maybe the act of observing Shabbat was the self-help mantra that would teach me how to have my own family.

After all these years, Judaism has brought tradition into my life. It's the banger single from *Fiddler on the Roof* for a reason!

Hearing Tevye excitedly sing about coming home to have dinner with his family always turned me on. If I *was* going to get married, I loved the idea of my husband working all week and then putting on a suit to have dinner with me and the children I bore for him. I wasn't crazy about the part in the musical where the wife had to cook the dinner, but that was before Postmates.

Unfortunately, there's more to Shabbat than eating challah and fucking your husband. You're also not supposed to do any work, which sounds great but is actually pretty complicated. The prohibited "work" includes all "deliberate activity." Apart from the basics, that includes: washing; plowing; lighting a fire; winnowing; threshing; weaving two threads; separating two threads; tanning; writing two or more letters; erasing two or more letters; transporting an object, either between private and public domains or over four cubits within a public domain.

I wasn't going to be the kind of Jew who would not tear my toilet paper squares after sundown on Shabbat. (Only the richest and luckiest Jews have gentile servants who will prepare their personal tissue for them.) Why can't I just do my own version?

My personal Shabbat is very customized. Basically, I do the dinner and the prayers, and then everything else I'd usually do during the week—except I try to turn off my phone from sundown Friday to sundown Saturday. If 90 percent of our lives is spent staring at our phones, a twenty-four-hour sabbatical from Instagram seems like the best religion any of us could hope for. Besides, I've never been someone to follow legalistic rules; if I knew what winnowing was, I would probably do it during Shabbat.

I like celebrating Shabbat with my family. And whenever I

participate in the Jewish holidays of introspection, I come out feeling better. I do, however, still have Catholic guilt about the fact that I don't go to synagogue more.

Synagogue was an improvement on Catholic mass, but I can't say I'm dying to go to the temple parts of *any* religion. I feel like it's a failure on my part. A prejudice maybe? Being thrown into Catholic mass at such a young age permanently scarred me. I remember the churches having the highest ceilings I'd ever seen and the priests and nuns being the most humorless and stern beings I'd ever encountered. The hours spent in mass during St. James Elementary are some of the most mind-numbing memories of my life. Old, unhealthy-seeming men in robes who didn't even appear to be nice people intoning scripture to a bunch of eight-year-olds? It must've been at one of these masses that I performed my first eye roll.

I haven't quite come to terms with how we will tell our daughter she can't eat pepperoni pizza with her friends because of our religion. After all, my husband's diet consists of: no pork; no shellfish; only kosher beef but regular chicken; fish that swim (but no swordfish—I guess they walk?); no meat and cheese together, but dessert with dairy after you ate a meat dish for dinner is okay. In other words, a hodgepodge of kosher rules and compromises he's concocted out of thin air and a copy of the Torah missing a few pages. I've always thought being an open and adventurous eater is a signal of open-mindedness and curiosity, and those are the types of qualities I want my daughter to embrace. How do I teach my kid to be religious in some aspects of her life but open and curious in others? I have no idea, but I'll probably read a self-help book to figure it out. At the very least, having to explain why she can't eat the rows of cured meats my father hangs in our refrigerator whenever he visits seems easier than lying to her about Santa Claus for twelve years.

Which leads me to the hardest part of being Jewish. The 100 percent worst part about converting to Judaism for me has been trying to erase the programming of Christmas.

The fever comes on around December tenth. I feel like there is some blood memory that exists inside me that wants to make ornaments and sing songs in my living room and put an orphan with a crutch on my shoulder. Even when I was a poor college student, I would always get a tree, paint ornaments and cards for my friends, and generally just feel more generous than usual. Don't get me wrong, I'm not such a basic bitch that I put a Rudolph nose on the grille of my car while I blast "Santa Baby"; but now that Christmas is out of my life, I miss it. It's like that hot, abusive boyfriend with the great record collection. I don't miss him; I miss listening to his cool records. (Ironically, I don't miss Christmas music.)

I grew up raised by a busy single mom, so Christmas at my dad's might have been our only family tradition. My dad must've gotten Christmas Eve with his family in the custody settlement, because even though my parents hated each other, I never missed a Christmas at his mom's house for my entire youth. Every Christmas Eve there was a party at Nana's house with my forty-five Italian cousins, where a drunk uncle would be Santa and every cousin would take turns sitting on his lap. One of my first memories is of swirling around at one of these Italian family ragers, telling jokes and discovering that I liked attention. (Should I thank these parties for my career in stand-up?) The point is, I did have at least one family tradition.

My nana's seven kids all had a bunch of kids and divorced and remarried and had more kids, and they all lived in the same town. And everyone came to her house for Christmas Eve. She would cook, and everyone would drink and smoke cigarettes and eat scallions rolled up in cream cheese and salami off of fancy glass platters. They would give Great-Grandma Lena the mink she always wanted, Frank Sinatra was always playing, and people were always swearing and fighting. It was like central casting for "typical Italian family," right down to the red velvet wallpaper and white marble statues in the living room.

My dad's side of the family always drove Cadillacs and had pools, and any money they had was gambled away in Vegas. (Maybe *that's* where I learned to live above my means?) But Christmas was our tradition, and it was fun—until about 9 p.m., when people started getting too drunk and accusing their spouses of cheating on them.

Now that I have a kid, I miss Christmas even more. I'd love to see it through her eyes. All due respect to the Festival of Lights, but there's nothing sadder than trying to get a kid excited about scraping together enough oil to light eight candles. Gather round, children, for a story about energy efficiency in ancient Israel!

I know Hanukkah isn't exactly supposed to compete with Christmas. Every Jew will tell you it's actually not an important holiday and they made up the present thing to compete with all the gentile children. (I'm paraphrasing.) Was there such a thing as Hanukkah spirit? And how was I going to get my daughter excited about it?

My child is obsessed with festivals and birthdays and loves any excuse to have a party. How do I shield her from Christmas and simultaneously get her excited about dreidels? Apart from a few episodes of Israeli *Sesame Street*, episode 504 of *Teletubbies*, and episode 27 of a cartoon called *Nina's World*, there wasn't a lot of Hanukkah content out there. Every episode we watched, the plot was always the same, with the same boring miracle: "We have to tell the rabbi we have enough oil to light the menorah!" Not exactly setting the scene for a winter wonderland.

I'm happy at least that I'll never have to pay scalpers' rates to get my daughter a VIP skip-the-line pass for a seat on Santa's lap at an outdoor destination mall. It always struck me as such a weird aspect of parenting that we are supposed to lie to our kids about Santa Claus. Fortunately, my daughter already calls Santa "that Christmas guy," so I don't think we'll have to do too much explaining.

"Why don't you just celebrate both?" my well-intentioned

friends will ask, as if I hadn't already thought of that. Unfortunately, my husband turns into Woody Allen with food poisoning at the sight of a Christmas tree. The first year we dated he came to my apartment and I asked him to hang the lights on my tree. Because the relationship was still new he did what I asked, but the whole time he was clenching his stomach, and I'm pretty sure he excused himself to go have diarrhea.

He's actually come a long way since then and now allows me to literally deck the halls with boughs of holly, aka put up garlands. Usually you can find them at the Christmas tree store and they still smell like pine in your house. (Probably 90 percent of what I miss about Christmas is the smell.) Considering that last year he let me get a Hanukkah bush, I figure I'll have an inflatable fleet of reindeer on the roof by the time my daughter turns twenty. Baby steps!

One night my husband was doing his evening ritual of "leaking" our daughter at midnight so she didn't wet the bed, and she said to him, "Dad, we celebrate Hanukkah but we don't celebrate Christmas." My husband proudly affirmed, "Yes!" She then said, "But, Dad, I am Christmas in my heart." My husband didn't tell me what happened after that, but I'm guessing it involved him using the toilet right after her.

In the end, maybe it doesn't matter if we run downstairs Christmas morning to rip wrapping paper off Walmart-bought presents (or, who am I kidding, presents from the artisan toy store in my neighborhood that sells mostly hand-whittled wood toys from Norwegian sweat shops). In my family the gathering of Christmas morning took the place of actual year-round closeness—it was a ritual that lasted exactly one day. Through the Shabbat dinners and Passover seders and, yes, even the Hanukkah candles being lit, we've crafted something that feels meaningful: a year-round tradition that will give my daughter a sense that we gather as a family to do these things. It doesn't much matter to me if she ends up Jewish—what matters is that she looks back and remembers that we did all this together. When she comes to me as a college sophomore having decided to convert to Sufism or become a Hare Krishna, I'll tell her that it doesn't matter what you choose—as long as what you choose feels something similar to Christmas in your heart.

INTO THE WILD,
OR GETTING YOUR CHILD
OUT OF THE HOUSE

"Never underestimate the power of stupid people in large groups."
—GEORGE CARLIN

When Riki Lindhome and I went to Uruguay, we stayed at this super-fancy hotel because our show, *Another Period*, had just been picked up for another season and we wanted to celebrate in the lavish manner we imagined our characters, sisters from Gilded Age Newport, would have.

It was the nicest hotel either one of us had ever been to. It seemed like there were more staff members working at the hotel than there were guests staying there. I remember dropping my napkin at dinner and two different waiters raced to return it to my lap, while another came from behind the wall with a mini flashlight to shine on the menu, in case the candlelight wasn't providing ample reading light. After we ate, our table was visited by a tea sommelier who informed us that Earl Grey was the "champagne of teas."

If you've gotten to know me at all by reading this book, you will recognize this hotel as my kind of place.

I assumed it was an adults-only hotel because the grounds were so peaceful and strewn with beautiful and sophisticated adults. Then we went to the pool, where we discovered a bunch of sixty-year-old ladies in white uniforms dangling steak into the beautiful guests' beautiful children's mouths. If there's one thing I learned from dating a billionaire in my twenties and also following Oprah's Instagram page, it's that really rich people make their staff wear uniforms, even if it's just khaki pants and a crisp white shirt.

Where were the parents? I looked to my left and there they were: wearing leopard-print bikinis and diamond toe rings, drinking whiskey sours and sensuously dancing to music playing at a frequency only the ultra-wealthy can hear. Meanwhile, their children were tucked away on the opposite side of the pool, being fed and entertained by the various staff these one-percenters had brought along with them, just in case the one-guest-to-three-hotel-staff ratio wasn't providing the personal attention/direct meat-to-mouth feeding their children required.

I didn't have a kid at this point in my life but I remember thinking that this scene was somehow both horrifying and aspirational. But mostly aspirational. I couldn't wait to not spend time with my child at a five-star resort in South America! Little did I know, however, that once you have a kid, traveling is only relaxing if you're rich enough to travel with an army of nannies.

It's enough of a production getting out of the house at all with your child. I remember a friend bringing her baby over to visit me one time—it might've been her first excursion out of the house with her baby ever—and she had brought so much stuff it looked like she had joined a traveling circus. Every new parent looks like a hippie on a Phish tour. It's impossible to look elegant when you're carrying four backpacks, and two of them are dripping applesauce.

Going places with your child is challenging. They need snacks all the time, they're easily distracted, and you have to always be prepared for them to shit their pants. The half of her life my daughter spent not in a pandemic, she still couldn't do much—taking her out was like taking a cat on a walk. And then, as soon as she could walk, talk, and use a toilet—or at the very least, tell me, "Whoops, I'm not going to make it to the toilet"—she had to stay home. Hey—better than a teen staying home for two years.

One of the perks of the early pandemic was that there were suddenly all these places you couldn't take your kids even if you wanted to (which you didn't). Chances are, you and your child don't have the same recreational interests. When the pandemic started, my daughter had just discovered Chuck E. Cheese and was asking to go there daily. I mean, it makes sense. I went there when I was little too. The Skee-Ball, the animatronic stuffed animals, the weird hourly ritual of the mouse "making it rain" tickets as toddlers scamper around on the disgusting carpet collecting them to redeem for plastic crap. These were all fond-ish memories.

I was happy for a break from pizza that looked and tasted like it had been made in a tire factory, but at the same time, my daughter had fallen under the sway of a much more powerful rodent. She wanted to go to Disneyland.

One of the challenges of being a person with impeccable taste in all things is that when you have a kid, you are now captive to the culture that your children consume. No childless forty-five-year-old knows what the hell CoComelon is. (I don't fully know what the hell CoComelon is and I've seen about two hundred hours of it.) No solo adult keeps PAW Patrol cotton-candy-flavored yogurt in her house. And Moana should have no bearing on a woman in the prime of her life, yet here I am, knowing all of the lyrics to "Where You Are." (Come on, that is a good song, though!)

I think I might be from the last generation of women who did not grow up wanting to be a princess. I remember wanting to be Janet Jackson or that girl from the Go-Go's. And I didn't become one of those adults obsessed with Disney either. In fact, I've broken up with two different guys because they took me to Disneyland for "fun." I spent the night with one of those guys at a hotel with paintings of the Seven Dwarfs on the wall, and let me tell you: nothing makes a woman hornier than a cartoon drawing of Dopey and Sneezy leering at her from above a faded floral bedspread.

I don't understand why everyone loves Disneyland. I don't

like long lines or cold turkey legs, and I don't think Cinderella's palace looks beautiful lit up at night because I've seen actual beautiful architecture. I wish we could divide up people between those who love Disneyland and those who don't and all the "don'ts" could meet—I bet we would all really love each other's company.

The problem with culture geared toward kids isn't simply that it's bad; it's that it's just a vehicle to sell stuff to the world's newest and therefore most gullible consumers. Slap a Disney character on even the most unappealing products at the supermarket and your kid will want to buy it. "Look, Mommy, that can has Olaf on it!" "That's dog food, sweetheart." "Okay. I want to eat dog food now."

The pandemic took family trips to Chuck E. Cheese and Disneyland off the table. But getting your kids out of the house isn't only about where you can take them; it's also about where you can drop them off. Yes, it was time for preschool.

In Los Angeles, if there is a philosophy, there is a preschool that adheres to it. French, Spanish, or Mandarin immersion. Reggio. Montessori. I toured them all. Would I drop my kid off in someone's backyard to play in a dirt pile or enroll her in a school with an on-site sushi chef and a "muddling station" where they can learn to make virgin cocktails?

Then there was the school that may also have been operating a pyramid scheme. The pitch was basically: come to our school and get 10 percent off hosting a party here (must use our caterers), or can we interest you in a VIP cubby for your little one for an extra seventy-five bucks a month?

LA even has preschools that are entirely outdoors. (If you tried that in Minnesota, 40 percent of the kids would freeze to death.) Outdoor school was an appealing option during the pandemic, but it can become hard to justify paying actual money to drop off your child in the middle of an empty field every morning.

Sorting through all my options, I discovered what I really cared about was limiting my daughter's exposure to technology. I blamed her iPad for bombarding her with commercialism. She seemed to think everything was for sale—she couldn't even read a book without going shopping for other books on the back of that book.

The entire world having a collective addiction seems, I don't know, dystopian and horrible? Everyone I know is fascinated by/ addicted to technology, from my three-year-old daughter to her seventy-five-year-old grandfather. Remember when we used to have elders and we relied on them for wisdom? Now when my dad comes to visit he just stares at his phone the whole time and thinks I will be impressed that the video of him dancing to "Old Town Road" just hit five views on his Jitterbug.

A little screen time is probably okay, but you always end up showing kids more than you want or more than you'd like to admit, or what you show them is just straight-up weird YouTube garbage. (Like everyone, I try to show my daughter curated Japanese children's anime, but she hates it.) When I'm alone watching my kid all day, we can go for a walk, go to a playground, do an art project, and eat seven times and there are STILL nine more hours to fill. So I let her watch three hours of *Barbie Dreamhouse Adventures* so I can focus on my own technology addiction, staring into the abyss of my phone.

I had taught my daughter to scream, "We don't want to buy your stuff!" at commercials when they'd interrupt whatever I'd put on for her on YouTube. We would make it into a game and laugh and scream at the TV or phone or iPad whenever they came on. She would often confirm with me: "We hate commercials, right, Mom?" "Yes!" I'd say. "They're the worst." I felt morally superior to every other parent until one day I was getting ready to leave the house and my daughter called out from the bathtub, "Where are you going, Mommy?"

"Mommy is going to be in a commercial, honey," I told her. My daughter's face fell. "Why are you going to be in a commercial? We don't like commercials, right, Mom?" Gulp. I felt worse than when I told her that I was thirty-two.

When I heard about the Waldorf school, the more I learned, the more I was sold. I even got my husband on board. (Or maybe he just didn't want to hear me talk about preschools anymore and pretended to agree with me.)

The main thing that attracted me to Waldorf, which starts in preschool but goes all the way through senior year of high school, was that they don't use technology. And that ban extended into your own home, so the kids grow up with very limited exposure to the internet and media generally. They don't have iPads, don't watch TV, and the parents all have to agree they won't "do" screen time with their kids, and as a result, parents can't have screen time around their child. (My husband, who has what I'd call a "robust online presence," was definitely not listening to me when I told him that part.)

These kids would never want to dress like a Disney princess, because they weren't allowed to watch Disney movies, or any movies. When I visited the school, I realized this Disney-sized hole in their hearts was filled in other ways, because literally every child in the schoolyard was dressed as a fairy, all of them carrying items like bows and arrows and homemade lutes. I visited during some kind of solstice party and the fairy children were zip-lining across the lawn to each other (yes, there were zip lines) so they could all sing a song to the fire gnomes before their afternoon snack.

The school was an elfin paradise. The classrooms were decked out in what looked like outsider art, and the textbooks lying on the desks had been hand-drawn and bound by the children themselves. Everyone's textbooks were different, based on their individual interests. As I toured the classrooms, I thought maybe I would've been interested in history if I'd been given the opportunity to illustrate my own textbook like these children. Maybe I would have been better at math and science if I were taught those subjects through dance, or "Eurythmy," a patented Waldorf movement-based teaching technique used in all their schools.

I thought if I could shield my daughter from growing up with a screen in her face all the time I might be giving her an advantage. If she never found out what a selfie was, she couldn't destroy her soul trying to become famous on Instagram, or destroy her body falling off a cliff so she could become famous on Instagram for a picture she posted of herself climbing a rainbow.

I felt like I'd become a prisoner to my own phone and I couldn't imagine what kind of effects so much screen time would have on my child's brain in twenty years. A Waldorf education seemed, frankly, magical. I would certainly be a different person if my public school teachers had treated me with wonderment and told me how special I was instead of barely tolerating me. I started to imagine a world where I sat by the hearth, finally reading *Anna Karenina* while my child polished her wooden toys on the rug that Moshe and I wove together one winter.

And then it hit me. I wanted Waldorf for *me*. Getting off technology was a dream of mine, not my daughter's. I wanted to go to fairy school where people told me I was special. It's hard not to see your kids as an opportunity to correct your own personal failings and live out your own unfulfilled aspirations. Was I going to stage-mom my kid into being bilingual, into playing an instrument (anything besides actual acting), into being a wood nymph who doesn't know what a cell phone is?

I also kept reading and learned that Rudolf Steiner, Waldorf's creator, believed not just in reincarnation but that the highest level of reincarnation one can achieve is as a white Aryan, specifically of Nordic and German descent. While they're no longer teaching his racial philosophies today, the preschool was a twenty-five-minute commute each way. So I was out.

So maybe the Waldorf utopia wasn't in the cards for me. I mean, for my daughter. But it made me wonder: Is a kid who plays with wooden toys hand-made by Danish artisans better off than a kid who plays with a plastic Peppa Pig you got for five bucks at Target? It's hard to know what's best for your kid, but one thing is for sure: you want them to be able to relate to other people in the world. "Where is your country house?" is not a super-cool ice-breaker for a toddler.

After all, what's the point of raising your kid in a diverse city if you're surrounding yourself with people exactly like you? Isn't that just like living in the suburbs, but with better tacos? If you're a four-year-old and you've never heard of the same things as everyone else because you've never heard of anything, does that make you unique and interesting or just kind of a tiny snobby dick?

Preschool wasn't going to insulate my child from all the negative influences of contemporary society. If we wanted our daughter to see, feel, and experience the world beyond her iPad, we couldn't just leave her with a bunch of rich white kids living inside a perpetual summer stock performance of *Peter Pan* (non-Disney version). We had to do it ourselves. (I know, right? Parenting is hard.)

For now, our favorite way to get our daughter out of the house is to go on camping trips. We're hoping that hiking in the woods and sleeping under the stars will give her a little bit of whatever it is she needs to be able to resist all the technology that will suck her in and make her want to buy things she doesn't need. And because my husband loves camping, she loves it. And I hope there are things she and I eventually do together (that aren't camping or even related to camping) that I love, and in a deep biological way she will love doing because we love doing it together.

But until then, I gave in and took advantage of a brief lull in the variants to take my daughter to Disneyland. Maybe what people love about Disney is that it does sort of act like a universal language for kids from all different backgrounds. Or at least that's what I told myself when a woman coughed on me in line for Space Mountain.

And while I wasn't crazy about getting my face scanned just to get into a theme park where I could spend thirty bucks on a Little Mermaid bubble wand that would break in my child's hand before we even made it back to the parking lot, I will say this for Disneyland: it is the only place I've ever seen a mother fill up a baby's bottle with Pepsi. Now that I'm a mother, I totally get it. Whatever works. RESPECT.

ONE IS AN ACCESSORY,
TWO IS A LIFESTYLE

"My child was a meaningful digression."
—ALICE WALKER

"One child? That is not a family!" my dentist exclaimed when I told him I wasn't having another baby. "Start trying right now."

"Uh, no, I'm good. I only want one. Life is hard enough without a double stroller and a Honda Odyssey."

"You're funny!" he said, not believing that I would actually only want one child. I didn't even want *one* for so many years, and the fact that I was even keeping her alive with the help of a full-time nanny was more than enough for me.

"One kid is like a Chemex pour-over. Three kids is a pot of drip," I told my dentist. "You're funny," he repeated, which is true, I'm a very successful comedian, but I guess he still thought I was kidding about having only one kid and was planning to have at least six more.

It's interesting to note that my dentist is male; I'm sure that if he had to extract milk out of himself in between filling cavities and giving fertility advice to his patients, he might be able to fathom a smaller family. (Observant readers will notice a theme of male medical practitioners giving me reproductive pointers with their fingers in one of my bodily orifices.)

I resented comments like these. As if "family" could only mean the scene from *Saturday Night Fever* with John Travolta screaming at his brothers and sisters across the dinner table, "The hair! The hair!" as he eats his pasta while wrapped in a tablecloth to protect his disco dancing outfit. Fighting over who got the last meatball was never something I wanted to re-create for my child.

People often dream of having a big family. Why can't I dream of having a small family? I feel like our family is perfect. If someone can think their family is perfect with two kids, why can't I think my family is perfect with one? I guess since I grew up amid a feeling of chaos, the civilized nature of a small family appealed to me.

Plus with only one, all of a sudden so many things seem more doable post-kid. A dinner at a nice restaurant, an impromptu trip to Puerto Rico, an oxygen facial while she sits quietly in the corner watching *Bubble Guppies*.

My husband always quotes me, "One is an accessory, two is a lifestyle," even though I keep reminding him I am not the author of this quote. I don't remember where I heard it, but it definitely rang true. And of course my child is more than an accessory and definitely more expensive than a Birkin bag (which she coincidentally fits into in a pinch).

In the old days, you could tell how horny someone's father was by how many siblings they had. My grandma had seven kids because my grandpa was horny. As much as raising multiple kids while consistently pregnant seems like a blast, something tells me that Nana would've loved to have been popping birth control pills. An average woman who got married before the 1960s was basically a peasant sentenced to a lifetime of ironing, lactating, and repeating whenever her husband got horny enough.

I love having one child; why do I need to have more? To be honest, the sibling emergency always baffled me. I have friends who, the moment they gave birth, started panicking about when the next child could be born. (Moms: The New Horny Dads.)

I couldn't imagine going back to being completely consumed by diapers, breastfeeding, and the sound of the pumping machine all over again right as my kid—who is already here and whom I love more than anything—goes through her cutest phases and my career possibly passes me by.

And I do this why exactly? So she'll learn valuable life lessons by having to share a bathroom with another child? Waiting for your brother to finish jerking off in the shower so you can get ready for school doesn't build character; it just makes you wear flip-flops when you bathe in your own home.

When I was growing up, only children were anomalies. There

was a consensus that they were psychologically a bit off, or at the very least, weird. They were like that because they didn't have anyone to play with (which also made them super-selfish because they never had to share), no brother or sister who tried to flush their head down the toilet when their mom left them alone for a couple hours.

Since then, ample studies on all those weirdo only children have found that they actually grow up to be more successful, smarter, and happier, and they make more money than people with siblings. So why the bad rap?

The data I read implied that perhaps the stigma of only children was contrived by capitalism to make people have a bunch of kids so they'll grow up to buy more of whatever is being sold.

Bill McKibben points out in his book *Maybe One* that only-children families on television are almost nonexistent. Meanwhile, I just saw an ad for a new show on Apple TV+, *Just the Forty of Us*, about a family with thirty-eight kids and they all need new iPhones every year.

Today, the more children you have, the more things they can buy. Kids used to produce for us; now we produce for them. The truth is we used to have large families because four of your kids would die after eating a bad batch of turnips or stepping on a splinter in your covered wagon, so you needed a bunch of spare offspring to help on the farm. Each kid could produce enough food to feed two kids, and even a four-year-old can shovel coal into the stove.

Back then, kids were producers more than consumers. And not to be too nostalgic about a time when kids began their logging careers at nine, all that consumption has a cost. Earth is kinda, I don't know, full? Environmental collapse is well on its way!

Sure, doomsayers have been wrong before, but eventually things will collapse, right? Isn't human overpopulation just a numbers game? It's funny to meet a mom who carries a metal straw in her purse to avoid the plastic waste but then has four kids. As I said, research has shown that having one less child is a more effective way of cutting down a person's carbon footprint than recycling, driving an electric car, being vegetarian, or replacing all of your lightbulbs with those horrifyingly bright LED bulbs that never need to be changed but make your house look like shit.

My friend with three kids wants to have a fourth. I asked if he thought that it was ethical to keep bringing more kids into the world. "Oh, the world needs more of my kids," he told me. "Ooooooo-kaaaaaaaaaay," I said.

Is my friend a closet eugenicist determined to slowly fill the world with his gene pool? Religious people have this many kids for precisely that reason. Get any Catholic or Hasidic or evangelical Christian man drunk and ask him why he has so many children, and he will most likely tell you he wants to populate the world with more of his kind.

But my friend wasn't that religious. And, to be fair, his kids are pretty cool. And smart. And champion social justice even at age ten.

The point is, he is raising his kids to be stewards of the planet and lovers of nature, to look out for the underdogs in life, to have a strong sense of self, to live their lives in a peaceful way, to be interested in other people. Plus, having four kids almost guarantees one will turn out cool. One can be artistic, one can be the scientist, maybe one will be the first billionaire environmentalist. And then you have an extra one who can be like, "I want to get a master's degree in improv, it's only seventy thousand dollars a semester" or "I want to move to Miami and become a nude DJ" and you won't care that much.

And that made me think. What if by having more kids I could increase my chances of giving birth to the next Greta Thunberg? Is each kid a genetic lottery ticket that will eventually lead you closer to your ideal child, or at the very least guarantee someone will be there to empty your bedpan when you are old?

And how do we make our only children not be entitled? Does it matter if your only child is more responsible for the earth if she thinks that earth revolves around her always getting the exact nut milk she wants? Not long ago my husband and I were on a walk with our toddler when she suddenly became inconsolable. We were both kneeling at her feet, desperately asking her how we could make her okay. Was she in pain? Did she have a rock in her shoe? Had the nanny given her vanilla macadamia-nut milk when what she really wanted was plain macadamia-nut milk with just a whisper of cinnamon? Did we have to fire another nanny?

We didn't know why she was crying, but for those moments, all of our energy as parents, our protectiveness, our attention, our love, was focused on this one tiny human being. We finally got it out of her. Her, and I quote, "Pine cone was too nature-y."

In China, where only children were pretty much the only children born between 1980 and 2015, the overindulging of only children is called Princess Sickness. (Just from the name, I already secretly want to have it.) All of the Little Emperors and Sick Princesses in China were the sole focus of their families. There was always money for what they wanted and they grew up accustomed to domestic help so that their parents could work. Sounds kind of like my kid, actually.

On the plus side, China's three decades of one-child policy are believed to have created the conditions for the country's massive economic growth and the reason I should've convinced my husband to put our kid in Mandarin immersion preschool. Add in way fewer millennials and a total lack of weird uncles, and it all seems pretty positive.

On the downside, parental preference for sons led to, you know, a lot of bad shit for baby girls. And now there are thirty-six million more males in China than females. By the end of the century, it's estimated that there will be seventy million extra men in China! (Maybe now they regret extinguishing all those females.) If America had a surplus generation of seventy million lonely single men, there would be school shootings every day. Interesting to note there are NOT more mass shootings in China. Turns out that lonely men don't kill people; lonely men with access to assault rifles kill people.

The truth is, there is no wrong family size. (That's also the tagline for the Apple+ show about the dozens of kids who now all also need Apple Watches and AirPods, and not the cheap ones, the good ones with adjustable sizing.)

So we'd all be wise to learn from each other's experiences. If you have multiple kids, the world can't stop when one of them is dissatisfied with a pine cone they picked up off the ground ten seconds earlier. That's a good lesson for us parents of only children.

And if you have an only child, they're not going to disintegrate into unloved nothingness if you tell them to leave you alone for a little while and go play with their brother, even if their brother is a rescue chihuahua that wears a shock collar because he bites both strangers and loved ones.

And who knows. Maybe one day I'll adopt and give up one of my fur closets. But for now, I'm not a kid person, I'm a "my kid" person. A second kid would just be tempting fate that I'd feel the same way about them as I feel about every other kid in the world (except for one).

BONUS QUIZ:
ARE YOU A ONE-KID PERSON?

- Could you care less what a baby's head smells like?

- Is the primary feeling you get from holding someone's newborn that your arm hurts?

- When you see a baby in a public place, do you never ask the mother how old it is, because you don't give a shit? (I am, however, curious how old the mother is: "Awww, she's adorable! How old are you?")

- Before you had a kid, when you would see a child making a scene at a hotel or restaurant, would you complain to the management? (Give yourself one point for pre-Karen days, two if you still do this and don't care if you end up on some rando's Facebook Live.)

- Do you only stay at adults-only hotels?

- When you see someone with a baby at the grocery store, are there no internal pangs, no biological ticking, in fact just a slight sense of pity for the mother trying to squeeze plums with a BabyBjörn slowly suffocating her? (Give yourself an extra point if you were happy when the pandemic made grocery stores adults-only.)

- Does being pregnant seem like hosting an alien?

If you answered yes to any of these questions, maybe just stick to one.

FATHERS ON MOTHERS, OR OTHER RECOMMENDED PORN SEARCH TERMS

"Marriage is a friendship recognized by the police."
—ROBERT LOUIS STEVENSON

Who knows more about motherhood than a father? He's been a punching bag in this book, much like the punching bag in his dojo, so let's see what a man thinks about motherhood. I thought it might be nice to have a conversation with my husband about parenting and motherhood—to see what a man has to say about all of this. He's always telling me how to do it, so I know he's an expert on it. I encourage everyone to read this chapter, then remark how much wiser I seem than him. With that, I give you the Karate Kid himself, the father of my child, Moshe Kasher.

NATASHA LEGGERO: *Hi, honey. I thought maybe I would talk to my favorite dad about motherhood.*

MOSHE KASHER: Dax Shepard wasn't available?

NATASHA: *He doesn't return my calls.*

MOSHE: So here I am.

NATASHA: *Okay, great. I thought this chapter was a good opportunity for me to passive-aggressively show you that I do more work than you.*

MOSHE: Is that a question?

NATASHA: *Ahh. A question. . . . Okay, here's one: How does your role differ from that of a mother?*

MOSHE: I guess I think of fathers as more of a primary caretaker role. And the mother's job is to observe and take notes on my form. I'm joking. How does my job differ from yours . . . ? [*At this point he takes a long, thoughtful pause, clearly terrified of what he will reveal should he answer honestly.*]

NATASHA: *We can skip it if you want.*

MOSHE: No, I don't want to skip it. I want to make sure I give you a thoughtful answer, and you can cut out these long, thoughtful pauses if you want to. Pablo, get down! You can cut me yelling at the dog too.

NATASHA: *Nothing's getting cut out.*

MOSHE: Okay, I think that the job of the mother and the father differs from family to family. But I think if I were to give some broad generalizations, which are generalizations about mothers, you know because they are broads?

NATASHA: *Stop deflecting with humor.*

MOSHE: Sorry, force of habit. I guess I'd say the mom tends to be the primary caretaker, organizer, and chief strategist. And I would say that the dad's job is CFO.

NATASHA: *What's that?*

MOSHE: Chief Fun Officer.

NATASHA: *Okay.*

MOSHE: But I also, and I don't know if this is a dad's job generally but it's mine specifically, is to act as a mooring influence on our family unit.

NATASHA: *Can you define "mooring influence"?*

MOSHE: Like, an anchor. Like, if I'm not around, I feel that you will float off into the ether of worry and anxiety. And my job is to remind us of the practical reality. But it's not just even about pragmatism. My job is to push our family into places that are adventurous and fun and aren't dictated by good ideas. They're dictated by—

NATASHA: *Bad ideas?*

MOSHE: No, but it's a search for fun and adventure and having experiences, rather than the search for, like, safety at all costs.

NATASHA: *Okay. That's interesting. Hmm.* [At this point, I must be frowning or sticking pins in a voodoo doll of Moshe I keep in my purse.]

MOSHE: Do you have some thoughts on my answer? It seems like you didn't like it.

NATASHA: *No, I liked it. Chief Fun Officer.*

MOSHE: I guess I'm also the disciplinarian-in-chief. It's like every time you lose a fight with our three-year-old, which is an area of endless amusement for me that you can somehow lose an argument with a three-year-old, and you come and say, "Moshe!" And I'm like, "Wow, this is like a sitcom." The mom is like, "Wait till your dad hears about this." And then Dad comes in and goes, like, "Don't do that!" And then . . . our kid listens to me.

NATASHA: *Oh, yeah, that's an issue. I shouldn't do that. That's a text-book thing. I'm working on that.*

MOSHE: It's not something you're doing wrong. It's, like, a dynamic. And might I suggest that it's possible that the dad acts as the disciplinarian because the mother has more responsibility. So it's almost like, "You know that mysterious guy that's not around much? I'm gonna call him—"

NATASHA: *"And he's gonna whup you."*

MOSHE: It's like you're calling the—the big guns in.

NATASHA: *And to be clear, we do not whup our child.*

MOSHE: We whup her mind.

NATASHA: *Okay, next question: Are you jealous our child loves me more?*

MOSHE: Is that a comedic question? I mean, obviously it is. But do you think that she actually loves you more?

NATASHA: *No, but I seem to be the go-to.*

MOSHE: The go-to what?

NATASHA: *When she's, like, "Mama, Mama. I want Mama to tuck me in. Not Daddy, Mama, Mama, etc."*

MOSHE: You think you're winning the desire race?

NATASHA: *Yes. Are you jealous?*

MOSHE: No. I have my own separate relationship with her that is different and has different energies and different vibes than the one that you have. So I don't think of us as in competition for a limited amount of love and affection.

NATASHA: *That's very evolved. Do you think you could have handled giving birth?*

MOSHE: Do you think you could have? Since you didn't?

NATASHA: *I gave birth!*

MOSHE: No, you didn't.

NATASHA: *I had my abdomen cut open and all my organs removed.*

MOSHE: Yes, I could have handled a minor surgery. But no, I don't think I could have handled vaginal birth. Do you think you could have handled vaginal birth?

NATASHA: *No, that's why I scheduled my C-section.*

MOSHE: Not to mansplain your own book to you—though this is literally the mansplaining chapter—but a better question might have been, do I think I could have handled pregnancy?

NATASHA: *Oh, okay. Let me ask you that.*

MOSHE: Nope. That I actually copyrighted. It's going in my book. [*Moshe demanded that I mention he actually does have a book, for sale right now, called* Kasher in the Rye: The True Tale of a White Boy from Oakland Who Became a Drug Addict, Criminal, Mental Patient, and Then Turned Sixteen, *available now on your e-reader. He's also writing a new one being published in 2023 and you should preorder it. And, with that, I have fulfilled my contractual obligation to him and do not owe him a fee for appearing in this book.*]

NATASHA: *Do you think you could have handled pregnancy?*

MOSHE: Great question. No, I really do not. I also don't feel like I could have handled the struggle you went through with fertility. That was very admirable and heroic to watch, how women—you specifically, but it's a women thing—get to a certain age, and sometimes it's not even a certain age, and all of a sudden your own body is telling you, "You're not capable of doing this thing that you're 'supposed' to be doing." And watching you go through that and struggle with the feelings of shame and sadness and heart-break that came with not being able to do it, and then courage and striving and stick-to-itiveness that came with continuing to try all of the different options. And the regimen of hormones and injec-tions and watching your body change. That was awe-inspiring, and I don't think I could have done that. And all that work and suffering is done in the name of what everyone knows will result in SO much more work and suffering if it's successful. It's not like once the fertility struggle ends, the work stops—if the struggle pays off, it's like you breathe a sigh of relief and begin eighteen years of the hardest, most consuming work you will ever do. It's like men get this two-year grace period from the labor of child-raising. So yeah, I don't think I could have done it.

NATASHA: *Okay. What is the main difference you saw in me when I became a mother? Be honest.*

MOSHE: Your breasts swelled and started producing a beverage. That was noticeable. Hmm . . . well, there are positive and there are less positive changes that I have noticed. I think you know that I think that you have become more worried as a result of having a child, and I think that you've made the argument that that's physi-ological, and you can't help it, and that might be true. I don't know the answer to that. But that makes me sad to see you having such a large part of your relationship with this miracle be one that's fraught with worries about the worst things that could happen to that relationship.

NATASHA: *It's not the worst things that could happen to the relationship, it's just trying to protect her. Because she doesn't have agency yet.*

MOSHE: But protect her from what? From the worst things that could happen to her? I mean, on some level I get it. Traditionally, couples have a worrier. And yes, more often than not, the worrier is the mother, but sometimes it's not. So I don't necessarily know that it's inherent to motherhood to worry.

NATASHA LEGGERO: *Well, I told you what I think. I think we're physiologically wired differently after we give birth to the baby. Like, as Judy Garland said, "Once you give birth, it's the same. You just now are living with your heart outside of your body."*

MOSHE: I feel that way too. I just am not, uh, constantly worried about a heart attack.

NATASHA: *Was your mother like that?*

MOSHE: My mother was loving to the point of suffocating. She loved me so much it felt like I couldn't breathe sometimes.

NATASHA: *I love our daughter that much.*

MOSHE: I mean, no, you don't, and I'm grateful for that. Because it didn't feel like love—it felt like lead. Heavy lead. Always there.

NATASHA: *What would she do?*

MOSHE: The way I describe my relationship with my mom is, I felt like I grew up with her sitting on my chest. She was just always there.

NATASHA: *Don't you think that we're always there for our child?*

MOSHE: There's a very big difference between always being there *for* your child and just always being there.

NATASHA: *Like, she just didn't let you go off and do your own stuff.*

MOSHE: It's not that. I had freedom, physical freedom, but I had very little emotional freedom. I just felt like my mom was sort of always . . . You know how when people play basketball, and they do that thing where they won't let you by? My mom was, like, playing hard-core basketball-defense parenting.

NATASHA: *Is there anything that your mother did when you were little that you wish I would do?*

MOSHE: I mean, yeah, she let us have adventures that weren't dictated by worries of disaster. She took us camping—

NATASHA: *Remember when you told me that she took you and your brother camping and he fell out of the top bunk bed and broke his neck?*

MOSHE: He didn't break his neck. But he was in a neck brace.

NATASHA: *I would have been too worried to let our child sleep on the top bunk of the bunk bed.*

MOSHE: See, to me it's worth the risk of a neck brace so that some-one can have the experience of sleeping on the top bunk.

NATASHA: *I'm just trying to keep her safe. Like, apparently many accidents with kids, fatalities, happen before age five because they don't know what they're doing. So I feel like keeping her safe during that danger zone period is of primary importance.*

MOSHE: Do you think that in fourteen months, which will be our child's fifth birthday, you'll pretty much stop worrying once that childhood-fatality danger zone has passed?

NATASHA: *I would hope that there will be some things that I wouldn't be so worried about. Like, if I don't find her in the house now, I start to get a little scared. 'Cause I'm like, "Oh, what if she wandered out the front gate and went into traffic or something?" I don't know. But I think when she's five, she might know not to do that. However, it could be, when she's five, she knows—*

MOSHE: She knows how to go to the street, put her thumb up, and get a hitchhiking situation going? My guess is that you will find your worry will morph into something else. To the reader—this is like our core parenting philosophical difference. And my argu-ment has often come down to the idea that worry doesn't actually help keep her safer. It just brings a pall of anxiety into her life. But it doesn't actually help keep her safer.

And that is the fundamental disagreement between our philos-ophies around anxieties around safety. I do not believe that imagining the worst-case scenario helps you make better decisions. Or I should say, helps *me* make better decisions. Because while you are busy trying to imagine the worst-case scenario for the thing that you're able to imagine—Covid, her falling off that cliff, or worse, a top bunk—another worst-case scenario that you never would've even considered is or could be happening . . .

The manhole cover flips up because a car drives by and cuts your kid's head off or, you know, there's a sinkhole in the sidewalk or a lion escapes the zoo and eats her—it's endless. Danger is infinite and there's no way to fully protect your child from danger through worry. The only way to offer any protection of your child from danger is to make reasonable, intelligent decisions, which you do, but surrounding those reasonable, intelligent decisions around safety, is doomsday, catastrophic thinking. Which I personally, I don't think helps. And I don't see any evidence it's helped our child maintain safety.

NATASHA: *Okay, so what would you say to someone who has a doomsday-thinking tendency, imagining worst-case scenarios? You majored in psychology. What is your prescription?*

MOSHE: I did not major in psychology.

NATASHA: *Oh, sorry. That was my ex-boyfriend.*

MOSHE: Uh, I majored in religion and so I would tell you to pray. But honestly. I actually think that prayer is not a terrible prescription for worry because—and obviously to some extent, this is very easy for me to say. I'm not a person who's prone to worry around this particular subject. I don't do doomsday stuff, not to say I never worry about our child, but it's not a big part of my conscious life with our kid, worrying about the worst things that can happen.

NATASHA: *What if you wake up, check the air quality, it's all in the red? Do you still go to a playground?*

MOSHE: If I do or don't go to a playground, it's not fueled by my imaginations of how terrible her lungs are gonna be. But if she goes out in the red AQI, and then she's gonna come home with a cough, then she gets bronchitis which turns into chronic asthma, wet pneumonia, systemic collapse, and then what if she has to be in an iron lung? I don't think like that.

NATASHA: *So you're not going to check the air quality?*

MOSHE: I guess that's right.

NATASHA: *Hmm.*

MOSHE: That's right, I'm not going to spend my time searching the world for potential catastrophes. But I am gonna be careful. Being careful is reasonable. Being overly careful is anxiety. So anyway, my point is, it's very easy for a person that doesn't suffer from that kind of anxiety to say—

NATASHA: *I never suffered from it before our child was born.*

MOSHE: Is that true?

NATASHA: *Yes. It's just about keeping her safe.*

MOSHE: Well, like I said, it's very easy for a person who doesn't have anxiety to say, "Just don't be anxious." But, in the same way, I have anxieties about other things, you know? Um, my career. I, I have anx—

NATASHA: *Death. You're afraid of death.*

MOSHE: I'm afraid of death. Definitely.

NATASHA: *But not afraid of our child's death.*

MOSHE: Yeah. Well, anxiety doesn't comport to, like, logic. It's just about—what's your worry. And I would say, honestly, meditation and, uh, and things like spirituality and meditation and yoga, and therapy, and self-improvement, and, hey, even prayer are probably the only way out of a cycle of anxious cyclical panic thinking. And I think there is a difference between my worries about death, my spiral thinking about death, and your worries about our child's doom. I identify my anxieties around death as unhealthy for me. They don't feel good. I don't defend them as actually possibly useful and virtuous. Because I think you can keep your child safe without worry and anxiety. However, I think worry and anxiety is a new danger that you've brought to your child's life. Because there is no possibility, it's not even close to possible, that your child will miss the fact that their primary caregiver is constantly worried about every step they take. There's no possibility that you won't transfer at least some of that anxiety onto them. And that is a new danger. One that you've introduced.

NATASHA: *I think that's a very good point.*

MOSHE: I would like to imbue her with the love of life, the love of nature, the love of experience, the love of knowledge, the love of culture, the love of music. The positive love of family, the sucking life down by the marrow, the being kind to others. The positive attributes of life, the giving, the fairness; you know, the kindness of life. The rareness of the opportunity to be alive. I want the positive parts, not the possible doom, the possible death, the things that could hurt her, the things and the people that could betray her, the money that could be stolen from her. Those aren't the foundation stones that I want to give her. Personally.

NATASHA: *What is the most impressive thing you think I have done in the capacity of mother?*

MOSHE: Um, I don't know. What's the most impressive thing you think I've done in the capacity of father?

NATASHA: *Well, this chapter's actually about me.*

MOSHE: I am curious though. What is the most impressive thing you think I've done in the capacity of father?

NATASHA: *You put your own desires aside?*

MOSHE: Have I?

NATASHA: *To, like, go take the kid to school or whatever.*

MOSHE: The most impressive thing you think I've done is . . . drive her to school? [*laughs*] Interesting. Okay, for you, I think that watching you come up with different things for her to do, activities, artwork, modeling music and culture to her, showing her about meditation and stuff like that. All of that is very impressive. I mean, obviously the actual physical ritual of carrying a child is the most impressive thing a man will ever see their partner do. But now that she's here and that is over, I would say, yeah, the way that you teach her about things that matter to you. I am not great at that. I try to have fun with her but I haven't yet figured out what things are "important" for me to teach her. You have such a clarity about that. I love to see it. Like from the very beginning of her life you would dangle high-end handbags in her face and teach her about the "big three" in fashion: Chanel, Gucci, Valentino.

NATASHA: *Very funny. Further question on the things I do that are impressive: Would you ever know where your wallet was or what the family schedule was if I didn't tell you?*

MOSHE: Here's what I will say. I don't know if our daughter would be in preschool right now if it was just me around. I've never looked up a preschool in my life. To this day. She's been in three preschools. I've never researched . . . I don't even really know what preschool is, to be honest. How long are you supposed to stay? I don't know how you get a child into elementary school. How do you get a child into school? Do you know?

NATASHA: *Not yet.*

MOSHE: But when the time comes, I already know you'll figure it out.

NATASHA: *Of course I will.*

MOSHE: And I'll be here to cheer you on.

NATASHA: *Thanks. Okay, next question: If you're using the washing machine, where do you put the soap?*

MOSHE: You pour it on the ground in front of the machine, right? And then ask it to climb in. Isn't that right?

NATASHA: *Where does it go?*

MOSHE: Where does it go?

NATASHA: *Yeah.*

MOSHE: The soap?

NATASHA: *Yeah.*

MOSHE: Well, it goes in the machine, Natasha.

NATASHA: *Where? Do you just, like, open up and put it in there, or—*

MOSHE: Do you think I'm, like, some kind of tailgater at a football game who just, like, goes to my union job and is like, "I don't know. That's woman's work. I never thought about it."

NATASHA: *I'm—I'm just asking because I do the laundry.*

MOSHE: It goes in the thing the soap goes in. The little tray that you pull out where you pour the soap into, and then you close it.

NATASHA: *That is correct.*

MOSHE: You know I was single for thirty years before we started dating, right? And that I didn't have dirty clothes on that entire time?

NATASHA: *I have my doubts about that. What do you consider a successful family?*

MOSHE: I think, like, a family that has fun together. . . . My family and I had fun together. I don't have this feeling of like . . .

NATASHA: *Heavy anxiety around your family?*

MOSHE: Right. I don't have that deep discomfort around my family.

NATASHA: *I like that answer because you don't hear about it a lot. And you know, I don't know how many people have that.*

MOSHE: I don't know either. I think people like their families a lot of the time. Don't they? For me, a successful family is that everybody's got information to share with each other. Like my stepdad is a scientist. My brother is a rabbi. My mom is a deaf woman and a teacher. And I am, um, a Hollywood triple threat. And so each of us is bringing some new bit of information, and we all have our roles.

NATASHA: *Did you always want to be a father?*

MOSHE: Yes, did you always want to be a mother?

NATASHA: *Um, no, I didn't, until I met you.*

MOSHE: Do you . . . does any part of you regret having kids?

NATASHA: *No.*

MOSHE: Like, zero?

NATASHA: *Zero. You?*

MOSHE: No, no. But I worry sometimes that my idea about having kids forced you into this life with our child that you love and are, are grateful for, but that it wasn't, like, what you thought you were gonna do with yourself or something like that.

NATASHA: *I can still do a lot with myself. I don't feel like life is over.*

MOSHE: But life is different.

NATASHA: *. . . There'll be new beginnings and life is different and maybe I'll have more time in ten years, I don't know. I mean, I don't feel like there's some sort of cap on anything that I'm doing.*

THE WORLD DESERVES MY CHILDREN

MOSHE: If you never wanted kids, why did you freeze your eggs?

NATASHA: *Because I am a very open person—you know, like, I never wanted to get a tattoo because I change so much, I'm always changing, I hope I'm always evolving . . . I like to learn as much as I can and change my thoughts on things sometimes. I can be influenced if I hear people from all sides, you know, I'm not someone who's like, I'm just gonna be this way forever. I feel like I'm always morphing and growing. So I thought, well, maybe there could be a day where I might change my mind and I'm sure it would have to be with a partner, and I was right.*

MOSHE: I'm glad.

NATASHA: *I am too. And part of me wants to say to people, "I feel bad for anyone who doesn't have a kid."*

MOSHE: That's a good message for your book. "I pity all childless people."

NATASHA: *I don't mean that.*

MOSHE: I know. And I do think that to some extent—we also had kids at the perfect time.

NATASHA: *What do you mean?*

MOSHE: Well, that's the thing about having kids late is that if you time it right you can have a child just as you start to ask yourself, is this really all that life is about? Is going out and partying and getting laid and going to the club and—hey, I like those things, but it feels like I've been doing nothing but that for so long. Right as you ask yourself: Is there something more I'm supposed to be doing? If you can time it right at that moment to have the kid, then you'll never have an existential question in your life about what you missed out on by having kids.

NATASHA: *But you may be technically "elderly" when they are in middle school.*

MOSHE: And dead by high school. Thus transferring the existential questions to them. See? No matter what you do—you're still going to ruin their lives when you die. So you might as well not worry.

NATASHA: *Or maybe worry so much that when you die it's a huge relief to them that you're gone. That's the gift I'm trying to give our child.*

MOSHE: I never thought of it like that. You know, you may be right. Well, look—you gave me a gift too.

NATASHA: *What's that?*

MOSHE: I'll give you a hint. She's screaming that she needs you to wipe her ass right now.

EPILOGUE

"We see that some people do not want to have a child. . . .
Dogs and cats . . . take the place of children. This may
make people laugh but it is a reality."

—POPE FRANCIS

I've just realized this book is mostly about me, as it should be. At forty-seven, I've accomplished a lot more than a three-year-old. From child "actor" (not child "star") to person on that great show that oddly got canceled to my dog Mayor Cutie having her own IMDB page, I thought I had done it all.

Before I had my child, I was content playing stage mom to a rescue Chihuahua with a bobbed tail. I taught her to jump through a hoop, roll over, and keep a wig on. I had her groomed, brushed her teeth, and even commissioned portraits of her. I had her DNA tested and found out she was half Shih Tzu, so I started treating her even MORE like Tibetan royalty. (Sorry to my other dogs, Pablo and Blanche.) I smuggled her on planes when I was playing places like the Joplin, Missouri, Laughter Barn (not a real place) and was low on money but wanted her cute little company on those lonely nights in a corporate business park hotel overlooking six freeways.

As we sat in bed, watching HGTV and sharing a salad, I thought my life as a mother was complete. I looked into getting Mayor Cutie cloned (if you're reading this, Barbra Streisand, call me) or at least eventually preserving her forever through the morbid magic of taxidermy, much to the horror of everyone I mentioned it to.

I doubted I could ever love a child as much as I loved Mayor Cutie. Then I had X2300!Mu$k and everything changed.

My daughter's birthday is February 23, 2018, which coincides exactly with the last day I ever brushed Mayor Cutie's teeth. Her teeth have mostly fallen out now, but the few that are left will remain unbrushed until she dies. I didn't clone her, and her daily incontinence on every rug is sometimes making me wish she would "wrap it up."

Don't get me wrong, I still love my dog. The fact that she's stayed alive for two years after being diagnosed with congestive heart failure practically proves she doesn't want to say goodbye to me yet. I thought being a dog mom would be enough for me, but then I became a mom to a human child and it was much more special. A great day with my dog is when she only pees on the furniture once. A great day with my daughter is when I feel like I'm in contact with an actual angel. And Cutie knows I don't love her as much as I used to, and not just because I used to play *Lady and the Tramp* for her and she remembers the plot.

I love my child in a way that I haven't loved anything else. She brings me so much joy and happiness, and, as I've said previously in this book, I don't like other people's dogs or children (including babies). But I only have to come into contact with my daughter for my mood to lift. She's like a human marijuana edible. Most of the time I feel like I've been given a gift to be able to interact with this little miracle who doesn't even know who Trump is.

When I look into her eyes, it feels like she is plugged into some kind of infinite energy. And it was fun to teach a human to walk. And not shit their pants. And then later teaching them everything a functioning member of society needs to eventually know. And hopefully when my daughter looks back on her childhood, she remembers me as a fun lady, not some buzzkill saying, "Don't throw sand. Don't throw sand. What did I say about throwing sand? Please don't throw sand, I don't want to have to ask again. Can you not throw sand?"

Am I just the lady who tells her dad you can't take a toddler to Burning Man, or buy her platform shoes so she can ride the rides she's too short for at Disneyland? I want her to know the fun side of me. How do I get her to know the part of me that was alive before she was born? The one who wasn't scared of anything. Did she die with my C-section? How do I model joie de vivre to my daughter when I'm in a surgical mask yelling at her to give the kids around her some space?

I love being a mother, but there are times when I'm so exhausted I beg my husband to put her to bed even though there's a 20 percent chance she could be tucked in wearing a ball gown, with scissors as a stuffie. Despite the fact that I feel totally physically and emotionally destroyed by a day of parenting, I find myself on my bed, trying to chill out for some me time, and all I do is look at pictures of my daughter on my phone. What the hell is wrong with me?

After more than four decades of doing whatever the hell I wanted, making someone else my priority is nice. I'm sure if I still woke up every morning and had nothing to do but attend to every one of my own whims, I'd be sick of myself by now. It's like a new challenge in selflessness. This person is so important to you that you can't fathom living without them, and at the same time, every few minutes (at least in the toddler stage) they potentially almost hurt themself. My child teeters on her chair every dinner, precariously close to leaning on the table and busting her chin or her head, and this isn't just because she worships my physical comedy.

You want to love and protect this thing that can't be trusted alone. She woke me up screaming the other night because she was shoving beads up her nose and they got stuck. She's almost four and really good at making beaded necklaces—I didn't know she had been hoarding some in her fist and I certainly didn't think she would stick them up her nose. As I tensed up and felt the tunnel vision come over me, with my hands shaking and her crying, I tried to remove the bead from her nose with tweezers, imagining the worst-case scenario. (Burst nostril? Bead-brain?)

I was out of breath; now we were both crying and scared. It's very annoying that the thing you love more than anything in the world, the person it's your duty to protect, the person you can't imagine living without, also shoves beads up her nose when she's bored. I will say, Mayor Cutie never did that. I do get why some people *prefer* the love from a thing that can't talk to you, understands only six words, and eats on the floor.

If you're looking for predictability in your parenting life, dogs are great. Over the last few years, Mayor Cutie has stayed waaaaaaay more the same than my little Musk-rat. Sure, she's lost a few teeth, but my daughter has grown teeth and will lose them, then her virginity, then she'll go to grad school and tell me she's a libertarian now.

My daughter has already changed so much just in the time I've been working on this book. When I first sold it, she was a baby who could only say "da-da." By the time I sat down to write it, she still wore diapers and had my signature "stick-straight" hair. Now I'm at the last chapter and she is a curly-haired full child with a large vocabulary who calls Christians "pork people." (Sorry, Pope Francis.) By the time this book is out in paperback, she might even be old enough to read it. (As long as she buys her own copy.)

With any luck my daughter will turn thirty, we'll smoke a

blunt, I'll nod supportively at the ultrasound of her baby's skeleton, and then I'll instantly die and never have to be called Grandma. That's got to be one of the perks of having a baby so late, right? Being called Grandma seems humiliating.

Maybe I didn't want to have a child for so long because being called Mommy is the gateway drug to being called Grandma. And, as embarrassing as it is, "Grandma" may be the best choice out there. There are so many terrible iterations of the word *grandma*, and your in-laws are going to want to experiment with all of them.

My Italian grandparents were called Nana and Papa (the rhyming version). But I've also heard the even worse Na-new (I think like the Mork greeting?) and Pee-paw (like when your dog pisses on your other dog's leg). My mother for some unknown reason wants to be called Grammy (maybe she loves *Gone with the Wind*?), which is worse than Granny but better than Gammy, I suppose? My husband's mom wants to be called Baba. My British friend calls hers Gan-gan, which sounds like a beast of burden from the Star Wars universe and doesn't sound cute even with a British accent.

If I do live to be a grandma, I hope my cyborg grandchild greets me with "Your Divine Grace, Natasha." I would even settle for "Madam." Or maybe my husband and I will love our child so much that when *she* has a baby, we change our names to Banma and Banpa. (Which is what I believe they call grandparents who are members of the Bloods.)

Getting old is rough. It's bad enough that you lose your teeth, hearing, eyesight, and ability to control your bladder, but then on top of that you have to be addressed as Meemaw. That's a fate I wouldn't wish on anyone.

I was certainly planning on outsourcing some of the time I spent with my kid in 2020, 2021, and currently 2022. The pandemic made me spend way more time as a mother and as a result, it's really changed me. At the very least it raised my tolerance for children in general. I've gained empathy for mothers on airplanes and won't sternly tell someone else's child to stop kicking the back of my seat anymore. And not just because airplanes have become lawless jungles where maskless passengers routinely punch flight attendants in the face during beverage service.

Waking up and throwing myself into someone else's life is now the norm. In fact, her presence made it extremely hard to finish this book by its deadline. Having a child is ironically the biggest obstacle to finishing a book about having a child.

Sometimes I will look back at a rushed morning and feel bad that I was being so stern with her. I want to be fun and in the moment when I'm around her. Am I being too annoying by telling her forty-five times to put her shoes on until I just do it for her? Was I too harsh when I begged her to stop sucking the sugar off of each Frosted Mini-Wheat and then flinging the discarded wet husk across the dining room table? Should I have just let her wear a swimsuit to school with hand-me-down moon boots that are still two sizes too big? And those are just three things that happened today before 8 a.m.

Parenting is consuming. The truth is sometimes I feel swallowed by it. But I love being around her. Every interaction has cute undertones, and I'm so excited for the person she is and will become. For example, I can't wait for her to become someone whose favorite song isn't "Gangnam Style." Yes, at the time of this writing, the PSY hit from 2012 is my cool child's favorite song.

For the record, I DID NOT play her this song. It's unsettling to realize that even with a three-year-old things will fall between the cracks and your child might find out about a viral hit from ten years before they were born. One minute, she's sitting through a full Neil Young song I'm playing for her. The next, she's moseying up to anything that even looks like a speaker and shouting, "Alexa! Play 'Whoop'em Gangnam Style'!" (We've had to remove the actual Alexa from the house.)

I had a plan for my child's musical taste and it did not include PSY's catalogue of one song. I try to ignore her as she dances around the house singing, "Hey! Sexy Ladaaay" but it doesn't help. I flat-out say, "That's a bad song, you should stop singing it, it's not cool," to which I get my very own personalized "Hey, Sexy Ladaaay!" I just keep trying to download other music into her head and hopefully another song will take the place of "Gangnam Style" before someone shows her the video and she realizes there is an actual dance that goes with it.

I know someone begging you to watch them jump on the couch to "Gangnam Style" doesn't *seem* like a fun time, but it's oddly rewarding. And I know she is going to like a new song soon, because she is changing every day.

And that's the difference between a dog and a child: you can't teach an old dog new tricks (well, I did, but it took a lot of broken hoops and ruined wigs), but kids are learning new tricks every day. And the best part is that you get to go on that journey with them—and then, if you're lucky, sell that journey as a sequel to your bestselling book about parenting. Due out in bookstores in 2026 (if the world doesn't melt by then)!

And to my daughter, I know you didn't ask to be born— although the chances of having you from sixteen eggs, to eight, to four embryos, to two, to one, to you—the world also deserved my child because you wanted to be here. You are the only magical being I've ever really gotten to know, and I love you! In fact I love you more than I've ever loved anything. More, and I can't believe I'm saying this, than I love myself.

Oh, and your kids can just call me Natasha.

ACKNOWLEDGMENTS

(If You're Related to Me and Reading This, Read This First)

I've never written a book and to be honest, I'll never write another one. It was too hard. So, to my family, if you're reading this, my only book, I'd like to say a few things.

Dad, people change. It's hard to know how to act when you're young. We just do what the people around us do. I love you and my daughter loves you. Thanks for being such a great Papa!

Mom, I'm a good mom because of you. You gave me opportunities and a good foundation and modeled behavior that makes me who I am. I know it wasn't easy, and you are so strong. I've definitely inherited that strength and am trying to model it for my daughter. Thank you for taking such good care of me—I hope I am doing the same for my daughter. I love you.

And to my darling husband, Moshe. You are always there for me and I love doing things for you. You're worth giving up Christmas for. I choose the spiritual and emotional tranquility of Judaism. I love when you come home because then I know the party is about to start. And you are not just fun, you are also a good person, and your ability to never tell even a small lie is aspirational. I am inspired by and in awe of your talents, ideas, and amateur plumbing abilities. I love you.

Thank you to all of the people who helped make this book better. My agents Steve Smooke, Cait Hoyt, and Anthony Mattero for helping me sell it. To Lauren Spiegel and Taylor Rondestvedt for being such engaged editors, the whole team at Gallery Books, and to David Parker for being a true creative partner on this book.